Tomorrow's Young Achievers

31 career defining insights for
a radically different tomorrow

Pushpendra Mehta

UNICORN BOOK

Publishers
UNICORN BOOKS
F-2/16, Ansari Road, Daryaganj, New Delhi-110002
☎ 23275434, 23262683, 23262783 • Fax: 011-23257790
E-mail: info@unicornbooks.in • *Website:* www.unicornbooks.in

Distributors
Pustak Mahal®
J-3/16, Daryaganj, New Delhi-110002
☎ 23276539, 23272783, 23272784 • Fax: 011-23260518
E-mail: info@pustakmahal.com • *Website:* www.pustakmahal.com

Sales Centres
- 10-B, Netaji Subhash Marg, Daryaganj, New Delhi-110002
  ☎ 23268292, 23268293, 23279900 • Fax: 011-23280567
  E-mail: salespmahal@airtelmail.in, rapidexdelhi@indiatimes.com
- 6686, Khari Baoli, Delhi-110006
  ☎ 23944314, 23911979
- **Bengaluru:** ☎ 080-22234025 • Telefax: 080-22240209
  E-mail: pustak@airtelmail.in • pustak@sancharnet.in
- **Mumbai:** ☎ 022-22010941, 022-22053387
  E-mail: rapidex@bom5.vsnl.net.in
- **Patna:** ☎ 0612-3294193 • Telefax: 0612-2302719
  E-mail: rapidexptn@rediffmail.com
- **Hyderabad:** Telefax: 040-24737290
  E-mail: pustakmahalhyd@yahoo.co.in

ISBN 978-81-7806-204-4

Edition: June, 2010

Printed at : Param Offsetters, Okhla, New Delhi-110020

Dedication

This book is dedicated to Young Minds across the world who I hope will bring in momentous changes in an increasingly small and "wired" world.

Contents

Acknowledgements

Done with my second book, thank you God Almighty, you made this happen.

To my nephew, Ajay and niece, Natasha, thank you. Through the world of gaming, you have taught me how imagination can be transformed into tangible success.

A debt of gratitude goes to my parents, Nirmala and Vijay, who encouraged me to write and make a difference in the lives of Young Minds.

To my sister, Malini, and brother-in-law, Vivek, I am deeply grateful. Your insistence that I study at Northwestern University was the turning point of my career.

To my brother, Sher, thank you for being a great source of continual advice.

I am grateful to Sonali and Balveer Kothari for being there on every step of the book's journey with creative ideas.

To my cousin, Ajay S. Mehta, I am deeply indebted. In 1994, as I was getting ready to leave for London, you quietly slipped

£100 into my pocket. In U.K., I used the money to buy a book on writing, which continues to hone my written voice as an author.

A special nod of gratitude goes to my cousin, Vikram S. Mehta. Your sagacious advice, "Education at a renowned US university will provide you the edifice to dream big and take risks" made my decision to go back to study only at an eminent university, very easy.

Thank you for your persistent reminders to complete this book: Rajiv Mehta (US), Ranu and Lalit Mehta, Tushita and Pradeeep Lodha, Smita and Amit Dhariwal.

Thanks ten million, Sheela Dalal and Zubin Patel. I couldn't have got my message through on critical HR issues, without your perspicacious inputs.

Many thanks to siblings, Aishwarya and Satyam Mehra. Your insights about the world of finance helped me communicate the bedrock of this project.

Thank you Jyoti Bhatt, an outstanding marketer, for reiterating that it is the 'Power of words' that is my differentiating factor as a professional.

I am grateful to you for providing specific contribution to this book: Amisha Shah, Amit Kakri, Christopher (Chris) Rathje, Freddie Pineda, Monica Marie Sanchez-Weglicki and Satish Kakri.

To Renee Appert, Katie Hulgrave, Kyle Parker and Lindsey Whately, thank you for teaching me the true meaning of creativity and innovation.

I am a better professional thanks to my ex-colleagues. It has been a privilege to work or interact with you. Thank you:

Brenda Shimmons, Christina Panay, Chuck Butler, Long Pineda, Tiodita Mori, Tanwi Tiwary, Jori Lynne Ortegon, Arati Gupta, Solymar Torres, Diwakar Ram B, Mathew Sangma, Bong Roxas, Siddhartha Chowdri, Rekha Dokka, Sambit

Lenka, Venkateswaran SS, Victoria White, Hannes Manndorff, Racine Ly, Felipe Mora, Fabian Serrato, Necia Stanford, Lynne Curran, Amitabh Saxena, Valerie Kindt and Alexandra Fiorillo.

I am indebted to the renowned faculty (past and present) at Medill School and Professor Daniel F. Spulber of Kellogg School of Management, Northwestern University. Your priceless insights helped me realize my true potential. Thank you:

Tom Collinger, Karen Brown, Clarke Caywood, Patricia T. Whalen, Lee Heubner, Jacquelyn Thomas, Edward Malthouse, Frank Mulhern, George Harmon, Nancy Hobor, Fred Crandall, Martin Block, John Greening, Paul Wang, Ted Spiegel, Don E. Schultz, Heidi Schultz and Daniel F. Spulber.

My classmates and friends from Northwestern University and Sydenham College of Commerce & Economics; I treasure our association and conversations, because you have helped me grow. Thank you:

Angela Piercy, Heidi Thompson, Michele (Castle) Long, Niya Moon, Candice Mims Dunn, Christine Jacobs, Dana Steinberg Abrams, Anup Samanta, Kerry (Lenahan) Y Fede, Anne Chen, Ali Chang, Nimisha Bajaj, Ramya Ramasami, Andrea Maher, Pamela and Andrew Davis, Christine Tabor, Zulfia Abdrashitova, Oscar Wang Ningzi, Yang Fengxia (Wendy), Lily Lee, Onur Kabadayi, Katie (Pratt) Rooprai, Caroline Kritzer, Katie Ferragut Colosi, Michele Silverman, Sage (Wagner) Wodarz, Jennifer (McDonald) Rowland, Julie Perkins, Jennie Greytak, Lilian Yu, Carrie Lin, Cindy Wu, Sylvia Chou, Todd Smith, Norio Imai, Youhay Miyamoto, Yunhui Wang, Alex Yang, Alice Lin, Alissa Kloner, Allison Masters, Alana Hartman, Ally Kuo, Ann (Graceffo) Ouimet, Ayako Ikehara, Divya Kumar, Elaine (Pescik) Mann, Elliot Campbell, Emily (Albright) Miller, Eunju Hwang, Geeta Chandan, Grace GuoYe, Greg Cordaro, Hsiao, Jeeyoung Hong, Johannes Jonsson, Joseph Fan, Julie Simpson, Kim Mogor, Lavanya Ramadoss, Madison Lee, Matt Imherr, Michael Cooney, Nantiya Borwornartsakul, Naeri Kim, Norio Imai, Patanasuwanna, Pasnai (Pat), Preeti Salvi, Priya Sanvordeker, Ramya Venkat Parekh, Reshma Khan, Rohini

Wangneo, Sara Adler, Shalin Kripalani, Swetha Yadavelli, Anil Bamboli, Harshavardhan Gangurde, Ravi Samtani, Satyajit Pendharkar, Rahul Gidh, Nina Ashar and Vikas Saraf.

Thank you Abhilasha Agarwal for your discerning insights that went into the designing of the cover.

Young Minds, I wrote this book as much in US, Peru, and international airport lounges, as I did in India, hoping that it will propel you to dream big in a small world, script your own professional destiny and inspire others to emulate your success. Cheers and smiles.

Introduction

I cogitated long and hard about how to engage Young Minds in a **'small, multi-tasking, short attention span, pre-occupied and digital world?'** After hours of reflection, my mind responded, 'Young folks, as never before, will be **most affected** by tomorrow's momentous socio-economic, cultural, political, technological, creative, legal and environmental changes.

The logical corollary–young minds would need to gear up to a world of insuperable pressure where they would need to make quick decisions about more complex issues in uncertain, rapidly evolving and competitive conditions.

'Hang on' my mind said to me.

'What are you going to say to your fellow young friends, who are far more intelligent, able, dynamic, and clear-headed than you, the author? What do you intend to share with super smart young jewels known in marketing and business parlance by different names–Genext, Millennials, Gen Why, Nexters, Net Generation, Boomlets, Baby Busters, or Me-Gen?'

How do you plan to involve and engage the young (I believe you are better informed than any generation that has graced our small world) that prefers omnipresent close buddies and dear companions as Facebook, Twitter, Orkut, Google, YouTube, Second Life, iPhone, iPod, iPad, Kindle, blogs, wikis, podcasts, gaming, webcam, net book, laptop, text messaging, camcorder, digital camera, and the online and mobile domain? The answer seemed rather clear-writing for this bright, ambitious, tech-savvy, enterprising, razor-sharp and independent minded legion would be a huge challenge... and yet my conundrum continued.

Do I delve on the pros of the diverse roles I have donned and attempt to strike a chord with young minds, because I am perceived as young, educated, pro-risk, exploratory, well travelled, and can understand their aspirations and mindset? Do I write about a world, which does not provide security of any kind–jobs, entrepreneurship, relationships or life? Do I focus on the multitude opportunities, choices and options that present themselves for millions of young minds, as never before? Or do I present a glimpse of the future where work and careers will be largely virtual, and driven by video based communications, printed books may give way to e-books, m-books, v-books and audio books, intelligent cars would automatically navigate street lights/traffic and obviate the need for us to be behind the wheels, high school graduation may happen at twelve years of age, and India may get its first 35 year old prime minister?

After much deliberation, I thought it is best to share with millions of young minds through this book, lessons acquired through my recent academic sojourn at Northwestern University and subsequent work experience encompassing anecdotes, observations, learning and explanations drawn from specific faculty members (past and present) at Northwestern University (Medill School and Kellogg School of Management), personal experiences, and conversations with successful classmates, associates and ex-colleagues that culminate into 31 career defining insights for young minds and their possible unlike endeavours—job and entrepreneurship, creativity and analytical pursuits, risks and happiness.

This I hope, will prepare young minds professionally for a diametrically different tomorrow, facilitate continual learning and change, develop a modus operandi (be it job or entrepreneurship) to prepare for the gloom amidst a boom, assist in adoption of bold steps to envision their place in history and reiterate the importance of making well-thought out choices to determine their future in 2025—15 years from now is not far away, but a moment in time with its crucial significance.

Given my record of professional mistakes and failures, lucky successes and divine intervention led attainments, unusual experiences, and exposure to some of the best minds in the mainstream and non-mainstream professions, including the only constant thing in my life–**preordained continual change**, I thought it best to collate my thoughts around the aforesaid occurrences and make a small attempt to sow the seeds of extraordinary success and greatness in high school, college and university goers, including young minds that are at an early or in a transitional stage in their professional careers.

Irrespective of the nature of academic pursuit (high school, college or university goers) or type of activity (mainstream or non-mainstream profession), young minds, I trust will benefit from ***Tomorrow's Young Achievers,*** which is an honest endeavour to create a better tomorrow for millions of young jewels.

I consider myself fortunate to have lived in 11 cities/towns within India and overseas. This provides me a tremendous advantage of relating to people from different countries as well as communicating with two Indias–The metropolitan and big cities with the exposure and better opportunities, and the small town India, which is throwing up unexpected stars across different domains.

After reading this book, in time to come, I hope the variance between the David and the Goliath will abate, and Young Minds, irrespective of region, city or location will tomorrow create a truly developed world. **Good luck and Congratulations in anticipation.**

Pushpendra Mehta
pushpendramehta@gmail.com

Chapter 1

It Takes Learning and Change to Tango

I think websites may cease to exist in the near future
Yeah....what's the need for a website, considering Facebook, Twitter and YouTube are great for promoting services and products!!

Chapter 1 It **Takes Learning and Change** to Tango

Learning & Change: Chief Change Officer or Chief Victim Officer.

"Learning and Innovation go hand in hand. The arrogance of success is to think that what you did yesterday will be sufficient for tomorrow."

William Pollard

"If you want to make enemies, try to change something."

Woodrow Wilson

A. What do I Know of Continual Learning and Change?

What do I know of learning and change? Am I erudite enough to write about it and influence young minds who I think are better informed than any generation that has graced our small world? NO. I am not wise, old, or a body of knowledge, but a hostage of 'compulsive change' that has lived in 11 cities/ towns within India and overseas, attended 10 educational institutions, bonded to create special friends across 18 countries, and sojourned through pricey boarding school, spartan paying guest accommodation, unadorned dorms, lavish apartments, and big houses.

If this is not enough, I have also donned diverse roles—*author, freelance writer, consultant, salaried 'job' professional and a new age entrepreneur*. My work experience encompasses marketing, public relations, marketing communications, negotiations, finance, strategic management, relationships management, analytics, creative writing, and the online and mobile domain. The left side of my brain loathes statistics, but thrives when the analytical bent of mind takes over. A penchant for creativity, ideas and dreams propels the right side of my brain, albeit my thoughts are ludicrous for most.

My change comprises extreme weather conditions, varied people, places and situations. At Mayo College, Ajmer (a small town in Northern India), for three years in middle (boarding) school, between the ages of 11-14, I have shared a big room with nine other classmates and two ceiling fans. The pair of fans saved us from the scorching heat that would envelope the town of Ajmer each summer. This was in sharp contrast to my unembellished small dorm apartment in Evanston (located just north of Chicago in United States) where the winter is severe and walking on the snow an art by itself. I was here in fall 2004 to pursue a Masters degree at Northwestern University.

After 10 years of work experience, I took a sabbatical to learn, unlearn and re-learn. My rationale for doing so, forewarned is forearmed—the world of tomorrow i.e. in 2025 will be diametrically different and envisioning the future with skills of today would be detrimental to my growth.

You could term my logic warped, because I am perceived as inconsistent, unsteady, inane, and exploratory. Perhaps, my predilection for the future, quest for continual learning, and rationale to brace myself for unexpected change lies in my upbringing. My genial father worked for a foreign bank and moved regularly between different cities, so my mother, siblings and I had no option but to move with him as most families would.

I changed schools regularly, and each time I made close friends the time had come to move. I realized very early that the best of friends will part. But I learned new languages, was exposed to different communities, festivities and cultures, and sometime during my childhood 'expected change' transitioned to 'habitual' change. You could argue that dramatic changes mean constant displacement, lack of focus or a difficult exercise to adopt.... I have a different story of my life that is replete with exciting anecdotes, noteworthy lessons and invigorating insights, to assist me prepare for the future.

My exposure to disparate people, places and situations is my biggest asset and motivation to change. Rapid moves from one town or city to another, has only created and fostered deep and meaningful relationships. I have a home with friends and relatives across 18 countries... and I am as comfortable in a simple apartment as in a luxurious haveli, with college goers or middle-aged people, a manual typewriter or my iPhone, a Windows enabled PC or my MacBook Pro, hard copy tomes or audio books, paper notes or Twitter, radio or podcasts, fax or Web 2.0 sites, a self employed or salaried professional, a maverick or a conformist, and more importantly with the underprivileged or the privileged. For a rapidly changing and Slumhope Millionaire world, my forte lies in my ability to live a line of Rudyard Kipling's beautiful poem *If* —'To walk with kings nor lose the common touch.'

I must confess my preference lies with the unknown, new and emerging, yet I enjoy the known, old and certain world. Was this mindset built overnight? Does this flexible disposition have any special connection with different segments or categories of young minds? Does the adaptability come with my free spirited and intuitive zodiac sign—Pisces? Am I spineless or unusual to attain the shape of water that changes its form with the type of vessel it floats in and out of, and yet it retains its quality to quench thirst?

The answers to all these inquisitions lie in the belief that continual learning and change abet growth and adaptability. To my mind, the strategic mantras to facilitate learning and change for young minds leading to 2025, which I shall elaborate shortly, are:

1. Playing safe is one of the biggest risks in the 21st century—Start early, start young.
2. Be yourself—build on your natural strengths.
3. Experiment outside your comfort zone or with a disregarded option.
4. Measure your performance each quarter.
5. Poach the career coach.
6. Reinvent via education: go back to school in your 30s.
7. Prepare to collaborate with the most unexpected.
8. Embrace flexibility—when a window opens up to an opportunity seize it.
9. Adjust to virtual and cross-cultural communications.

As a child I was made to undergo rapid adjustments and sweeping changes—some I resisted or abhorred, the others came naturally to me. Are unexpected adjustments, swift modifications, continual learning or planned changes good or bad; a strength or weakness? By the end of the chapter you can decide this for yourself.

Today's world will be different from tomorrow's. I wish to continue being in the learning mode, because by 2025, the world will witness epochal changes and I much rather look at my laurels rather than rest on them. 2025 is knocking on our doors. It is almost here and preparing today for professional survival, success or excellence for a date 15 years from now may seem absurd, but necessary.

Today, if you are 15 years old, you will be 30 in 2025, and if you are at present aged 40, you will then turn 55. In 2025, you would still be part of the professional circuit, but whether you will be contemporary or obsolete in your chosen profession will depend on you and your attitude. You may respond, 'that is a no brainer.' After all you will never allow yourself to get jaded or archaic. Welcome to reality—look around you and you will see a large number of educated people in their 20s, 30s, 40s and beyond, who are behind the times or outmoded, and have little idea where to go for help or what to do to get on with the times.

Just as today's technology will not work tomorrow, our present skill levels or attainments will not see us through 2025. Only an inclination for relentless learning and perpetual change will help us win the battle of 2025. Yes, the great battle is not with anybody else. Your competition is with your future in a small world. We have all grown up so fast, and 2025 will be here as swiftly as the time we take to bat an eyelid.

I am by no means an expert on futuristic developments. I am only attempting to share a sense of what to expect and prepare for with my 'fellow' young friends, as we usher in a future, where our vehicles will monitor the safety of our homes and our refrigerator will dig into its database and based on our consumption patterns and social calendar, inform us of groceries we need to buy for the week.

There is only one thing constant from here on... the battle of 2025 will be won through a repetitive, frequent and constant learning mode. Hopefully, 15 years from now, young minds will transform our small world and preside over it in different fields.

***

B. Young Minds & 2025—Insecurity Creates Incredible Opportunities.

We are living in a world, which does not provide security of any kind—jobs, entrepreneurship, relationships or life. This explains why insurance companies and banks love our wallets.

Young minds, as never before, you will be most affected by enormous socio-economic, cultural, political, technological, legal and environmental changes that shall engulf your personal and professional life. Welcome to a world of insuperable pressure where you would need to make quick decisions about more complex issues in uncertain, rapidly evolving and competitive conditions.

You are inheriting a world where personal relationships are being questioned, existing business models are not providing significant results, ubiquitous technology is altering social and cultural behaviour, online and mobile commerce are changing the way payments systems evolve, a legacy of environmental degradation is beginning to endanger eco system, technology cycles are getting shorter, and the advent of 'new age' saboteurs, fraudsters and terrorists is threatening to take over our financials, privacy, social and communications network.

But every negative has a positive, every problem presents a solution, and every adversity provides an opportunity, which is why you are also a part of exciting times, where perhaps, for the first time in history 'the world of internet and cell phones' has created a level playing field between the big and the small; where it takes individuals with comparatively less money to create a Google; where a job loss can be a great funnel for dreaming big as an entrepreneur and generating employment; where the consumer knows more (knowledge is not just power, but supreme) than the employees of an organization; where old and traditional media conglomerates can be challenged by start-up online and mobile media ventures; where old adversaries are new friends; where in a digital economy, people want to communicate, and collaborate with others across seven seas; where real money is being spent to buy virtual goods; where a mobile phone acts as a TV remote or a movie projector and also stores money; where Twitter, LinkedIn, Second Life and Facebook have made the world a smaller place; where YouTube can be your voice of self expression and cash machine; where a library of audio books, m-books, v-books and e-books on your cell phone or laptop may supplant paper back or hard copy printed books; where 75-100 year old venerated companies are unsure of survival; where blogs, digital cameras, webcams, smart phones, net books and podcasts are creating a new wave of media reporters or citizen journalists; where the spread of WiMAX, 3G, 4G and

Web 3.0 will revolutionize news, information, communications and entertainment; *where the young can achieve stardom early and easily; where it does not take 30 years to make a difference or be a billionaire....but this is only the beginning of the change that will be a part of our lives by 2025*.

Mastering the 'art of incessant change and flexibility' will be critical to your success. This will come about only if you are ready to start making small changes NOW, if you acquiesce to reinvent the wheel, and treat accolades of yesterday as bygones, and failures as a necessary facet to greatness.

My father who is the offspring of the Second World War generation, always felt until recently that his generation had witnessed *'unparallel'* changes through the mediums that facilitated sweeping social order makeover... telegram, fax machine, television, photocopier, scanner, cash register, computer, calculator, credit card, ATM, advertisements and power point presentations.

He candidly admitted to me a few years ago, "Today's change is bigger than yesteryears. You cannot allow yourself to feel I have arrived in life because upon graduation, I got a better job than my classmates. You cannot bask in glory after securing admission to the best college or university in your chosen avocation. You cannot blow your trumpet for outstanding results attained by your organization last quarter... that quarter just ended yesterday. You cannot lean on your innate blue blood or silver spoon to hold sway. You cannot feel privileged because you got professional recognition rather early. Triumphs are short-lived in the 21st century. The winds of change can knock your accomplishments very soon. Keep on learning and changing before they fire through the range at you." Dad's thought provoking observations comes from his inclusive experience in various capacities within the profit and non profit world. He prefers to interact with young minds, because it keeps his learning process ignited.

***

Young minds are inheriting a world that does not provide security of any kind—job or entrepreneurship!
Which is why every adversity and uncertainty provides a revolutionary opportunity!
And in such exciting times you can even create or surpass a Google with less money.

1. Playing Safe is one of the Biggest Risks in the 21st Century—Start Early, Start Young

Kyle Parker is a successful entrepreneur, and one of the most intelligent young professionals I have met in my life. He attained a Masters degree in Integrated Marketing Communications from Northwestern University, and is president of a marketing and business channel development firm representing manufacturers in the video surveillance and Homeland Security industry. He has served as a broker's assistant in the US Treasury Bond pit at the Chicago Board of Trade (The world's oldest futures and options exchange) and was also very active in state and national level political campaigns.

Kyle recently founded www.securityspy.tv—a video blog and social networking community for professionals involved with cyber warfare and cyber security. I have admired Kyle for several reasons; primarily because he is an interesting conversationalist—that comes from being intelligently curious, a voracious reader, an eloquent public speaker, and an early adopter of new technology and consumer electronic products. Kyle is extremely open to diverse cultures, and his impeccable sense of humour can breathe life into the dullest gathering.

In 2006, Kyle told me, "Playing safe is one of the biggest risks in the 21st century. Just as ships are not built to stay in the dock, we are not meant to stay where it is safe. We have to face and cross choppy waters to stand tall in a new world where the rules of the game will mandate recurring risks for survival." He reiterated this sagacious advice to me during my last trip to US in 2008.

Kyle quizzed me once, "Pushpendra do you know why Steve Jobs, Bill Gates, Michael Dell, Sergey Brin, Larry Page and Mark Zuckerberg were able to create iconic brands as Apple, Microsoft, Dell, Google and Facebook?"

I thought I knew the answer (I was wrong) and yet I said, "Why Buddy?"

His answer was not what I had in mind. It was remarkably simple yet worthy of note. He replied, "Each of these luminaries took risks when fresh and young, when the burden of the word *experience* was unknown to them. It is easier to take risks when young. Even if you fail, it is better to fail early than late. Young risks do not have to worry as much about reputation. Older risks have to worry about image management."

Kyle and I have often deliberated the concept of early adoption of risks by youth. We have often discussed the pros and cons of exploring unchartered paths when young. We have often cogitated about the importance of moving outside the comfort zone when young. We have often pondered about the impediments of playing safe when young... it provides for a safe haven in the short term, but creates more obstacles in the long run when the world around us changes rapidly and threatens obsolescence. We have often mulled over the journey from oblivion to greatness... and we have arrived at a debatable conclusion, but something we are convinced about—Get out of your comfort zone and take risks - start early, start young. You have that many more years to bounce back or change course should things not work out as planned.

And should it work out as you envisaged, you will have that many more years to assist or serve your family, organization, community and nation.

To my mind taking risks commences with taking small steps to confront your fears. It is ambling towards small measures of indulgence with the unknown. Go back to the first time you were asked to jump in a pool and try swimming. You may have been scared, but you did it. Go back to the first time you were asked to drive a car or ride a bike. You were nervous, but you did it. Go back to the first time you participated in a school play, public speaking competition or a musical show. You were shivering, but you did it.

In each of the aforesaid occurrences, you took a small step outside your comfort zone, you took a small risk, you failed the first time, but you bounced back and learnt swimming, driving, acting, music and public speaking. You managed to acquire new skills because you were in the learning mode, because you were raw, because you were sharp and quick on the feet—all done most comfortably when you are young.

One of the best ways to face up to unknown challenges, and take small strides towards a risk-enhancing appetite is to live overseas or internationally for at least a quarter. Preferably, do so when in college or university.

Volunteer to teach a language or a creative course, learn a foreign language (Spanish in Spain, Chinese in China, and French in France), study in an exchange programme, work as an intern, backpack and travel by yourself or live with an 'adopted' family. There are innumerable options for college and university goers to live abroad for a quarter or semester.

Alternatively, if you are an entrepreneur or employed with an organization, look out for the earliest opportunity to work with people from other parts of the world. You will broaden your horizons, learn to spread your tentacles and risks, hone your cross-cultural, networking, relationship and professional skills, get prepared for an increasingly globalized and small world, and remain forward-looking. Remember, learning is a two-way process, and when you work with foreigners, they will also learn and grow from working with you. And if you become friends, future visits to each other's land will be that much more special and highly cherished.

During the early part of my consultancy career, I was fortunate to have worked with some of the brightest minds from North America and Asia Pacific. As I acquired more experience and was exposed to work practices of other countries, I grew exponentially as a professional.

There have been moments of anguish, frustration, differences and conflict in cross-cultural assignments, but each time I was presented with an opportunity of getting out of my comfort zone to work with people from another country, I chose to grab it with both hands, because leadership dexterity, cerebral depth, networking ability, communications versatility, art of tact and persuasion, strengthening of functional competence, anticipation skills and operational acumen were heightened and augmented.

Spend a quarter with a foreigner on a work project, extracurricular endeavour or academic assignment and you will be a positively different person. Explore these low risk options and it will change your perspective about life. More importantly, it will introduce you to a new person – YOU that you may not be aware off.

***

2. Be Yourself: Build On Your Natural Strengths

When I see an eight or nine year old operating a smart phone, computer, iPod, or video game, I am often bewildered at their dexterity with hi-tech gadgets and gizmos. Even though, I am into gaming and live by the online and mobile world, I wish I was 20 years younger.

I also ask myself why is that each generation is considered smarter than its previous generation? Why is it that the future overrides the past and creates its own communications and social networking style?

The answer may perhaps lie in the Hindu 'Theory of Reincarnation.' As an example, he who died in December 2000 and was possibly reborn in January 2001 was already exposed to computers, internet, cell phones, video games, and the rapidly changing world in the year 2000. In the present incarnation, he would have carried forward from his previous birth his knowledge, attitude, temperament, beliefs and skills, which may delineate why a young kid takes so naturally to electronic gizmos, gadgets and technology. It also alludes to the importance of building on your natural strengths, talents or competence.

Observe a child who is outstanding with computer or video games. The child in his relentless pursuit, attempts to better

I am an ideas and creative person, and can even sell a comb, to a bald man. Yet I am stuck as an accountant!
Then you should pursue marketing, advertising, sales, media, or public relations. Get Going!

his last score and set a higher bar to attain the next time around. The child is 'preparing' himself for greater heights in the world of gaming. During this process he or she gets completely involved, oblivious to the surroundings or the clamour around him or her.

The act of planning, strategizing, repetition, innovation and hard work, perhaps unknowingly fuse, to help the child attain a new personal record on the computer or video game. More importantly, the mental gumption and determination to succeed is phenomenally high. All this happens because the child is 'naturally' focused to excel at gaming thereby building on his or her innate strengths, talents or competence.

Even a child prodigy exudes certain 'inherent' characteristics or talent for a particular craft (music, entertainment, painting, sports, dancing, and writing) or vocation. These inborn traits were tapped early, which is why the child became a phenomenon. The actions of the past were understood and developed to create a child sensation.

As we age and face the compulsions of the material world, how many of us pursue as an occupation or career that we are naturally good at or inherently gifted with? We let our natural talents and strengths go untapped. We do not focus on what we can do best or what is the 'right fit' for us. We focus on what society determines is appropriate for us. We work hard and long hours, and yet find large number of people disengaged or frustrated with their workplaces.

If you do not have a natural affinity for numbers, and have yet acquired an accountancy degree or an MBA in Finance, you may do well, but are unlikely to be a great accountant or finance czar. If an individual is gifted with words, creativity, ideas, and selling skills, he or she would much rather pursue marketing, advertising, sales, media, public relations or a non mainstream profession as writing. Instead we find the same person languishing in production, operations, or analytics. We are attempting to be somebody else. We are forgoing the opportunity to contribute more. We are embracing short term success for long term greatness. We are allowing our true potential to remain dormant.

Today, animation and gaming has become a great career choice, but 10-15 years ago we would have mocked at somebody who adopted it as a career. Why? Because society's rules, options and material demands bind us to follow what our peers pursue or chase careers unsuited or misfit for us. We build on our weaknesses and yet rejoice at our career choices because we have a cool looking car (on a car loan), a big house or apartment (home loan), big bucks (our money is not with us but in a bank, mutual fund, insurance company or stock market), and the latest electronic gadgets (3D, LCD or Plasma TV, smart phone, and an expensive laptop) ...but what differentiates you from the rest – your colleagues, friends, family, acquaintances and associates?

Try this today. Go to a beach, lake, ocean, sea, forest, garden, or a silent corner in your office or home. Rewind life, and ask yourself these questions - what were or are my strengths that I can build on naturally? Did or do I excel in writing, painting, music, photography, public speaking or some other craft? Was or am I the lord of numbers, analysis or gut feel? Do I enjoy playing safe or love adventures and risks? Did or do I have a special affinity for the underprivileged? Did or do I like to dream and build projects? Did or do I like to lead or follow? Have I ever successfully sold a product or service and did I enjoy the process? Am I passionate about a particular line of work and can I dedicate my life to it?

Once you become aware of your natural strengths, you can commence the pursuit of your true calling. Look around you, within your family, friends, relatives, colleagues, associates and acquaintances—you will find far too many people who have either spent a lifetime in the wrong profession or chasing somebody else's dream. If you focus on your intrinsic strengths, competence or talents, and go after it fervently, you will never feel jaded, mismatched or disengaged. Life will then become more beautiful and meaningful.

Heidi Thompson works for Sojourners, a national faith-based advocacy organization in US. She is a wonderful person, compassionate, caring, generous, well read, intellectually curious, and an able leader. Heidi has an innate strength - predilection for writing and dedicated service to faith-based organizations through fund raising and marketing.

She identified her natural fondness for the written word, marketing and fund raising, and enrolled for the Masters degree in Integrated Marketing Communications at Northwestern University. Heidi's larger motive to go back to school after years of unswerving commitment with faith-based organizations was to bring cutting edge marketing, analytics and communications practices to their world and make a bigger difference.

Heidi knew the importance of 'building on her natural strengths and competence'—writing, marketing and fund raising skills. She focused and worked hard to harness her strong points through her academic sojourn at Northwestern University. She underwent courses that would strengthen her skills encompassing marketing management, consumer behaviour, customer contact and database marketing, analytical techniques, public relations, marketing public relations, investor relations management and crisis communications, among other discerning courses that lead to the successful attainment of a Masters degree.

Upon graduation from Northwestern University, Heidi integrated her adroit writing skills, with advanced marketing, analytics and communications knowledge to get hired as a Director at Sojourners. Today, as Chief Marketing Officer at Sojourners, Heidi manages the organization's brand and all earned-revenue activities, including an award-winning magazine, and an e-commerce site.

With 15 years of fundraising and marketing experience, her enthusiasm and positive energy radiates professional fulfilment. Change is a continual process for her, simply because she adopted newer learning with a focal point, and practiced hours, months and years to sharpen her natural strengths and skills.

The rule of 'building on your natural competence, talents or strengths' is a prerequisite for changing with times. The possibility of embracing change is easier when you focus on developing your key competence or strengths for social change, personal elevation or material aggrandizement. We forget the story we heard as a child that in our professional quest, the tortoise can beat the hare. Life is a long term contest and those who focus on their natural strengths; set high standards and then work feverishly to chase their bold dreams attain pre-eminence.

***

3. Experiment Outside Your Comfort Zone or With a Disregarded Option

We live in a world of specialization, where our experiments may be restricted to our area of expertise or interest. But a small experiment outside your comfort zone or with a disregarded option (with your complete commitment), particularly during college, university and the early part of your professional career, may prove to be rather beneficial in the long run.

While in college or university, you may have as a major or specialization—mathematics, computer science, business management, psychology, sociology, history, economics, statistics, sports, fine arts, writing, theatre or music. You may also have a small list of your favourite and less favourite courses (courses you dislike). It is imperative to spend the greater part of your time and effort in the area of your specialization, excellence or passion.

However, for courses that seems boring, irrelevant or lacks any immediate benefit; consider pursuing at least one of them with absolute dedication and interest. If you are pursuing engineering take a course in sales or marketing. If history is your major consider doing a course in information technology. If economics is your first love, go in for a course in psychology. If creative writing and you are best friends enrol for on online media and web marketing course, and if you deplore statistics as much as I do, get cracking buddy and spend a quarter or a semester understanding regression or survival analysis. Yours truly did sleep with his adversary (statistics and analytics), fairly recently at Northwestern University.

As you move on in your career, the same engineer who thought sales or marketing is irrelevant, will need it on the job to sell his idea or as a budding entrepreneur called to develop a sound business plan. The same historian may leverage information technology to create an online social network of historians. The same economist will be far more accurate with his GDP forecasts as he integrates his projections with consumer sentiment resulting from an understanding of people psychology. The same creative writer will need a personal website, blog or podcast and search marketing skills to effectively brand and communicate his work. The same professional who hated statistics now needs it to comprehend web analytics for his online venture.

What you consider unrelated or dreary today, may be vital for your success tomorrow. A small experiment with a course outside your comfort zone or a disregarded option, will not only be a knowledge enhancing exercise, but also make your profile more marketable in future. Remember, experiments of the past can help you in the future. What is inexplicable today may explicate itself tomorrow.

While pursuing my Masters degree at Northwestern University, I was 'pleasantly coerced' to experiment outside my comfort zone by Renee Appert. She exhorted me to enrol in for a quarter long course in Investor Relations Management (IR), yet I was not convinced.

It is very difficult to win a discussion with an intelligent woman who is a creative genius and has a heart of gold.

You know her considered opinion has merit to it and she will make waves upon graduation from the Masters programme in Integrated Marketing Communications at Northwestern University. Don't believe me read on...

Renee *currently oversees the branded websites and digital media programs for the world's top appliance manufacturer*. She is a thought leader in emerging marketing communications that appeal to today's consumer. Her aptitude in interactive media, passion for cause marketing, and creative zest has resulted in a unique blend of fruitful results.

In 2006, Renee successfully established Habitat for Humanity's largest annual brand-sponsored blitz build, which has received seven industry awards to date. She is presently engaged in developing new digital pathways for manufactures and retailers to unite in the online shopping process.

Renee has an undergraduate degree in Fashion Design and Marketing Communications from The Fashion Institute of Technology. Away from her laptop, Renee is an accomplished international marathon runner (she has promised to come to India to run a marathon), appreciates modern art and loud rock music.

Renee did make use of her silent yet subtle persuasive power to make certain classmates pursue the path to creative self development, when she was convinced that her suggestions will enhance their professional pursuits. But in spring 2005, I did not see any reason in enrolling for an IR course. I knew my finance and did not see myself as a Chief Financial Officer or Chief Public Relations Officer with a transnational company. Additionally, I had plans to pursue a far more relevant course—an e-commerce planning and marketing module.

Renee did not give up. She appealed to my ego and said, "Pushpendra I see you as a CEO of a reputed company and IR then will be a logical corollary to comprehend." She expounded how IR would enable me to understand the nuances of Sarbanes-Oxley, Regulation Fair Disclosure, corporate governance, stock-trading, financial communications, road shows, annual meeting, and the makeup of business ethics while managing the stakeholders of a company.

I thought to myself, "I am an ethical person and have a strong value system in place. Road shows, financial communications and stock-trading may never be a part of my primary job, so why should I trade e-commerce planning and marketing for investor relations?"

My nature to experiment took over, and I 'condescended' to Renee's persistence of pursuit of investor relations. She had a theory that crisis, greed, frauds, scandals and failure will recur in the world of business, and knowledge of investor relations management will be vital to hone our leadership skills and better protect the community. Then, we were in the year 2005 and none of us knew about the global economic crisis that was to unfold in a few years.

Unexpected change and stress had become a part my academic life. Our IR class was held in the evenings and ended at 9:30 pm. This meant a change in work plan (and late dinner) for the entire quarter. However, the course was worth its weight in gold.

We were exposed to some of the best minds in financial communications. The faculty and the guest speakers were outstanding. The course was a great combination of academic and pragmatic practices of investor relations management. Today, I cannot thank Renee enough, because the course opened my mind to the vastness of investor relations, importance of financial jurisprudence, and how successful and ethical CEOs, CFOs and CPROs operate to adroitly manage their diverse stakeholders, including the board of directors.

As a dream big entrepreneur or an ambitious top management aspirant, you will need the same investor relations skills that Renee was persisting about, when she convinced me of enrolling into a course, which I thought was irrelevant and unnecessary for me in spring of 2005.

Today, I can better understand and communicate the economic crisis of 2008-09. Renee Appert was right... crisis, scandals, failure, greed and frauds will recur. In the beginning, experimenting with a disregarded option or outside your comfort zone is uncomfortable, but at the end the heart swells for having achieved a staggering task with varied positive ramifications. Not to forget that the résumé becomes more saleable and the knowledge bank also broadens.

***

4. Measure Your Performance Each Quarter

In fall 2004, Prof. Tom Collinger, Associate Dean, Medill School and Chair of the Integrated Marketing Communications (IMC) programme, Northwestern University, imparted to me an apparent, yet overlooked beneficial insight for continual learning and change—'Measure your performance each quarter.'

Tom Collinger, who additionally serves as Associate Professor and Sector Head of Direct, E-Commerce & Search Marketing at the IMC programme, is a widely recognized expert in marketing management. He has served as senior vice president of Leo Burnett Company and general manager of Ogilvy & Mather Direct. I was in the presence of a marketing and strategy genius.

Prof. Collinger, enunciated his thought, "Pushpendra ask yourself key questions each quarter—Have you fared better than the previous quarter? Do you know more than the last quarter? Have you grown since the last quarter? If the honest answer is a definite 'yes' you are in the learning, growing and changing mode. If the answer is 'perhaps, may be, unsure or no,' then it is imperative to start working right away to make the answer yes."

You may ask me, "Is it possible to grow each quarter?" The answer as Prof. Collinger told me then and is as relevant today is, 'Yes, it is possible.'

What I understood from his astute remark, I wish to state—growth each quarter may not always be in terms of enhanced grades, revenues, profits, salary, bonus or promotion. It could translate into more knowledge, wiser experiences or an improvement in skill set pertaining to your profession (doctor, accountant, lawyer, reporter, writer, painter, photographer or architect) or organizational function (marketing, finance, strategy, human resources, public relations or production). Once you are aware of the importance of growing each quarter, you move to the next step—you ask yourself tough questions and get candid answers that determine your performance in the present quarter.

For each of the inquisitions provided below, compare yourself with the previous quarter:

- Do I know more about my profession?
- Have I worked harder or smarter?
- Have I benchmarked myself against my biggest competitor (your future is your biggest competitor)?
- How far have I gone to implement the views of the gurus and achievers of my profession?
- Did I try and work on at least one path breaking idea?
- Did I try and unlearn and relearn during this period?

Answers to these questions will provide you a qualitative and quantitative appraisal of your current progress and aid in measuring your performance each quarter.

"Corporations and enterprises measure their performance each quarter. Individuals need to do likewise. The earlier you start measuring your performance each quarter, the faster you will become your personal change agent," Prof. Collinger said.

The brilliant words from a venerated professor had opened my mind to a new way of adopting learning and change.

Organizations work to increase their revenue and profits each quarter. We too can learn each quarter, grow each quarter, read more each quarter, listen more each quarter, enjoy more with our family and friends each quarter, and smile and reach out to more people each quarter. Qualitative aspects like happiness and joy will manifold. Quantitative metrics as better grades, more money, deserved promotion, and increasing profits will follow too.

Somewhere, somebody in India or some other part of the world, is working to drastically alter the business, technological, scientific, creative or analytical practices that we are used to as students, executives, professionals, entrepreneurs, or academics.

Revolutions and innovations are known to transform established methods and construct new paradigms, which in itself are not permanent. Today's Facebook and Second Life will be passé when the next wave of social media introduces the next big innovation on the internet and mobile media space.

Those who wish to envision the future and continually anticipate, adapt, innovate, create, and reinvent their mindset and skills are destined for greatness as long as they remember to put into practice the wise words of Tom Collinger—measure your performance each quarter. You will then be able to change prevalent techniques and make history—faster and smarter, and for the better.

***

5. Poach the Career Coach

I have always admired the creative and sports world for a multitude of reasons, and what it highlights rather effectively is the importance of a 'mentor or career coach' for our professional growth. A mentor or career coach teaches us humility. Humility creates opportunities, because we listen more. And should we go wrong (everybody makes mistakes)

I possess multiple skills and that means more choices. Should I become a marketer or a consultant, or perhaps an entrepreneur?
We all need an **independent and neutral** voice to point us to our true calling. Go and speak with a Career Coach.

they guide us through the mess... as long as we are open to suggestions.

We all need an external, higher, or experienced impartial force to aid our professional development. I recommend every young mind wishing to make it big in the professional world (job or self employment) to preferably, get a mentor, career or executive coach early on in their career. The seed for distinction as a professional genius is best honed by the preceptor. The advisor could be a career or executive coach, your teacher, professor, current or ex-superior (boss), colleague, friend, associate, acquaintance or a friend's 'parent or sibling.' It is best to get a coach or mentor who will be nonaligned and not get shrouded by coloured opinion about you. Parents, siblings, cousins or extended family can act as a wise guide, but it is not easy for them to be objective or neutral, and offer advice that recommends hard choices.

In 2005, I was trying to map out a suitable career for me in the 21st century. I was inclined towards marketing, financial services, management consultancy, internet and writing. Even if I wished to, I could not have then integrated them all. Sometimes if you possess multiple skills it provides greater choices. Choices mean you have acquired more knowledge and possibly, the pragmatic tools to execute. But choices also lead to confusion (wouldn't mind such confusion). Angela Piercy my classmate at Northwestern University showed me the way.

Although, Angela and I possess wide-ranging work experience, she is far ahead in terms of intelligence, emotional depth, exposure, values and inner gumption. She was the person I would turn to for advice on career planning. Angela had observed closely my strengths and weaknesses, and when asked to, would voice her independent and dispassionate opinion. She is not a judgmental person, but an astute reader of human psychology. I never told her then but she became my career coach and confidante.

Angela and I would discuss a range of topics—business, government, environment, community service, marketing, public relations, marketing communications, investor relations, crisis management, books, spirituality, religion, values, ethics, relationships, careers, global mindset, etc. We had our lighter moments too. I never lost an opportunity to pull her leg and trouble her with my mischievous jibes, but as gracious as she is, Angela always laughed it off.

In 15 months, Angela knew me as well as few do, and recommended a 21st century career in 'creative writing, media, marketing, public relations, marketing communications, academia, consultancy or services oriented entrepreneurship.' Each of these careers she felt would allow me to self express my views with or through the power of the written word.

Angela had become my mirror. She had analyzed my profile and sized up my academic and career attainments, including interests, circumstances and the future. Her incredibly well coined advice gave my career a new direction. Angela and I are miles apart, but in a wired world my professional coach is just a few minutes away.

The enormity of change leading to 2025 will transform the world around you. Your achievements may not count tomorrow or your one big success may wipe out repeated failures of the past. Your ground-breaking creation may be consigned to history or you the nonentity today could become a part of the celebrated tomorrow.

Different scenarios will emerge in your professional life. My observations have taught me a fundamental truth—it is difficult to ask for guidance when you are successful, highly educated, arrogant, famous, self-opinionated, or going places in the shortest possible time. No matter how intelligent, knowledgeable, successful or gifted you are today, an *'objective, sagacious or experienced' coach + the smart young you'* will make a better duo to brace up to the challenges leading to 2025.

A good coach is somebody who is well read, inspires you to dream big and attain great heights, exudes positivity, has the ability to pick you up from the rubble should you falter, keeps you grounded when recognition comes your way, thrives on change, accords values and ethics its due importance, sparkles with clarity of thought, believes in true education, exposure or travel, propagates an unconventional mindset and does not hesitate to give an honest and independent opinion. Look around you and away from you, and you will get your professional or career coach. Remember, even the super rich and discerning CEOs continually look to their coach for strategic advice. The first Chancellor of the German Empire, Otto von Bismarck once said, "the main thing is... to make history, not write it." A coach can help us to make history. Go create history with your career coach.

***

6. Reinvent via Education: Go Back to School in Your 30s

The advent of cable television, DTH TV, IPTV, smart phones, internet, emails, m-commerce, social media, Web 2.0, 3G, digital signatures, wireless, Wi-Fi, WiMAX, among other astounding innovations has completely changed the way we pursue creative and analytical vocations.

Unlike renowned writers or authors of yesteryears, a modern day creative writer or author has a savvy website or blog. A reporter, who started his or her career with fountain pen and typewriter, has transitioned to a laptop, net book, digital recorder and smart phone.

Increasingly, every creative vocation is becoming a business, and even non-profits (NGOs) all over the world are embracing sustainable development, technological proficiency, and new age communications, business and marketing practices, to continue making a difference in their stakeholders lives and causes they serve. 'Reinvent via education' is a novel mantra, because rapid change is moving in from all directions.

Education, your new age long time date or spouse requires a makeover continually. He or she has to be bribed and wooed... again and again to rake in the *moolah*, create new success stories, make a difference or stand out in a crowd. Education broadens our mind and creates a common ground to connect with motley of people.

In the 90s, a few days before I graduated from my alma mater Sydenham College of Commerce & Economics, Mumbai, my father forewarned me about the outcome of impending globalization, internationalization and the march of technology that would envelope every arena—creative, academic, sports, politics, spirituality or business, among others.

He said, "Those born in the 70s and thereafter will need to study twice to stay with the times. Your first advanced degree (Masters or PhD) will be attained in the 20s. But as you move on, that education may not be adequate cover to secure the next three decades of your chosen occupation. You must be prepared to go back to university in your 30s. The battery titled 'career' will have to be re-charged or reinvented in a decade, perhaps in your early or mid-30s by the pursuit of a second Masters degree. Renewing yourself will provide you with new ideas, exposure to global developments in your profession, access to best minds and practitioners in your avocation, opportunity to understand emerging trends and accurately anticipate the future." Dad was spot on.

Guess what? With the passage of time he forgot the sagacious advice he imparted to me, but I followed his counsel and after 10 years of varied work experience, took a sabbatical in August 2004 to pursue a Masters degree at the hallowed Northwestern University, considered among the best universities in the world for marketing, communications, media and international business. It epitomized the canons of education – concentrations, faculty, location, and reputation. My re-birth and resurgence after an onerous journey was waiting to happen.

Back to School in 30s—The First Pain that I Fell in Love With

The first month at school was tough. It was like walking on the snow with bare feet. Reinventing was a nightmare. I wondered, was my Dad wrong and did I have to redefine myself? I was doing fine in India and was used to regular media coverage on views pertaining to retail loans, plastic money and online financial services.

Friends and family would be elated to read my quotes in the prominent publications of the country. I gave up the recognition to go miles away, where I was a non-entity, burning the midnight oil between study material, papers, projects and reports. Did I shoot myself in the foot? For me the overwhelming challenge was to get back to student life after a hiatus of 10 years as a visible professional. The clothes had changed, the walk was different, and the pay cheque had stopped. After a decade, the first month as a 'returning' student was terrible. It was baptism by fire.

'Business Statistics' the course I always detested was as ever beyond me. 'Consumer Behaviour' the foundation of marketing made my coffee and pizza breaks longer. 'Marketing' that was at my fingertips as a former marketing specialist, worked differently for me as an academic course. Many a sleepless night was spent trying to fathom new age marketing concepts and quantitative equations that were being disseminated to prepare us for an extremely analytical business world.

'Finance' as an academic module and *The Wall Street Journal* was the saving grace, albeit it did create time management issues as some my fellow classmates did seek my regular inputs to understand the world of numbers or quantitative complications. Coffee, chocolates, anecdotes and jokes helped the self-anointed finance assistant to work with his apprentice. You have the edge if know your finance and accounts.

Reinvention comes with pain... it never is easy. And the first grey hair because of academic stress and crazy study hours worsens the feeling. You create a positive feeling around the solitary grey hair—you give it a name, Wisdom. But pain brings with it a heightened calm, an inexplicable self belief and the necessary knowledge base for the 21st century that tells you, 'Yes, you are ready to take on the evolving world.'

A gruelling yet joyful journey at Northwestern University ended in December 2005. I graduated with a Masters degree in my 30s and was chosen to make the conclusion speech (write and deliver my own speech) at the graduation ceremony of the Medill Integrated Marketing Communications Programme. As I walked to the podium to address a large gathering, I was a very proud young global citizen.

It was an honour and privilege to make the closing remarks amidst a big gathering that had congregated from different parts of the world. Elation had taken over the built up exhaustion that comes from the pursuit of a challenging advanced degree at a top US university. Yet another young mind was walking out with his head high.

The 15 months at Northwestern University were intensive, but special. The IMC programme has taught me a futuristic approach to integrate business and creativity with marketing, finance, analytics and communications. The IMC degree has built an edifice that allows me to explore options; a structure that enables me to take risks and anticipate the unexpected.

Overseas education inculcates a deep appreciation for cultural divergence and richness, where you devise your own technique to overcome language and cultural barriers, and also understand that... language and intelligence are not correlated. In the 21st century, the power of the digital economy and education, and the rise of BRIC (Brazil, Russia, India and China) countries will result in increasing social alliances and cultural exchanges among the most unlikely ethnic groups.

Individuals who delineate skills to overcome cultural, cerebral and linguistic barriers will have a definite advantage. My sabbatical at Northwestern University has equipped me for new age social, cultural, creative, business and spiritual connections.

I underwent an arduous journey of learning, unlearning, and re-learning... miles outside my comfort zone and in an extremely competitive milieu. Easier said than done, but made possible because of the fear of being outmoded, the curiosity to probe the unknown, the opportunity to grow and anticipate the future, not to forget the allure of making friends across diverse continents. I feel re-invigorated, energized and 10 years younger brimming with new dreams, aspirations and hope. I am born again with more ideas and energy.

For somebody who believes ardently in the accepted notion that the world is a great university, and there is no substitute to real world experience, I am also of the opinion that scholastic attainments, academic courses (short term or specialized) and on-going education provides a framework to our big ideas, an ability to bounce back with renewed dynamism, the security to take a risk and move back to a safe zone should things not work out, and the necessary knowledge to get into new areas or change businesses.

Pedagogic achievements cannot supplant basic intelligence or guarantee successful execution of a brilliant concept or idea, but it can augment professionalism and enhance the possibility of making a successful transition to a drastically different tomorrow, directed by a digital and knowledge based world.

The years 1999-2009 have taught me an important lesson, which I have cogitated ad nauseam, and wish to share with my fellow young brethren—all of us have to be prepared for an economic downturn or slow down once every decade or sooner. Every few years, we have to be prepared for new business models and adoption of shorter bench life technology. We have to be prepared to accept that the learning acquired during the pursuit of our graduate or post graduate degree may not be good enough to support our entire career. Our answers to excel in this fleeting and technology driven world lie in our ability to continually upgrade and re-learn.

Going back to school may be a great way to combat the forces that induce uncertainty or insecurity and embrace change for a prosperous future. Remember, investment in education is an investment in yourself, and an investment in yourself will shape the destiny of you, your family and the future generations.

***

7. Prepare to Collaborate with the Most Unexpected.

The interactive, virtual and mobile world is creating a collaborative mindset. It is weaning away individuals and enterprises from the old school 'dog and bone' syndrome. The word 'compete' has a new ally, 'collaborate.' The future will be about forging alliances and partnerships with colleagues, friends, acquaintances, associates, and companies. More than ever before, unexpected deals and grouping will take place. Astounding collaborative scenarios that may be scoffed today may occur tomorrow... Google and your start-up mobile commerce venture may work together on a new mobile payment or m-retail product. Facebook and your three employee garage operated digital media agency may work together to develop a path breaking business model for new media. *The New York Times* may get all its Indian content from your early stage media company. Harvard University may collaborate with your little known alma mater to set up a virtual university open to students from all over the globe. Amazon.com may work with your five people 'editorial and publishing' team to develop audio-books and e-books. An international telecommunications company may work with its sacked (ex) employee to develop the next generation of video mail and messaging. The CEO of a big company may work as a head of a division in a competitor company. You could be hired by your mentee and have to work for him in a new formation or venture that promises to redefine the animation business.

Changing times means changing equations and new connections. This requires a mindset that is beyond hierarchy, power, class and social structure, and ready to collaborate with an unknown entity, unimportant group or emerging association. You must remember that it was individuals with no entrepreneurial history or 'big' corporate success behind them who created acclaimed companies like Infosys, Google, Apple, and Microsoft. They have taught us that the unknown, the unimportant, the small, the emerging and the dark horse can turn big, and change the world around us. And by 2025 what will take you to the top will be your willingness to successfully collaborate and work with people within your company, outside and across regions—familiar and unfamiliar, new and established, creative and analytical, maverick and conventional, occidental and oriental, good and great.

Start disengaging from the stereotypes (hierarchy, titles, power and control) we hold close to our chests. Size will not matter. Tomorrow's world will be much different—the famous will take the first step to collaborate with the unknown, the emerging, and the unimportant. Remember a Nobody today will rise and become a Somebody tomorrow.

***

8. Flexibility—When a Window opens up to an Opportunity Seize it.

Lao Tzu the founder of Taoism and the author of *Tao Te Ching* said, "Men are born soft and supple; dead, they are stiff and hard. Plants are born tender and pliant; dead they are brittle and dry. Thus, whoever is stiff and inflexible is a disciple of death. Whoever is soft and yielding is a disciple of life. The hard and stiff will be broken. The soft and supple will prevail."

Lao Tzu defined flexibility brilliantly, and delineated the importance of a pliable mind. You have two options—an inflexible or rigid stance or a flexible and adaptive disposition. An inflexible stance means you are so set in your own ways that you cannot see any other way of doing things. A flexible mindset denotes a continual contemplative process of examining state of affairs and situations, anticipating futuristic developments and then swiftly adapting to changing circumstances. Flexibility is a virtue because it seeks options and is quick to seize opportunities. Inflexibility a weakness because it does not wish to give up fixed methods that lead to missed opportunities.

Flexibility starts and ends in our mind. We can be as pliable as we want to be and open ourselves to unknown or unconventional experiences (that may seem bizarre to the onlooker) or prefer the status quo as a sign of smug self-satisfaction. Flexibility means adoption of the trial and error method or following an unbelievably strong intuitive gut feel, almost inexplicable at times. Flexibility means an ability to adapt to unexpected situations and not be unduly concerned about society's expectations. Flexibility is what allowed Steve Jobs, Bill Gates, Sergey Brin, Larry Page, Michael Dell, and many others to give up their proposed course of action to pursue their true calling. Flexibility also means letting go of an idea, project, or premeditated pursuit if it is not a suitable match.

Dana Abrams my classmate at Northwestern University learnt her first career lesson early—be flexible. Her professional life amidst the US economic downturn is upbeat, because of her malleable mindset. You may think she is ambivalent. I think she has shown tremendous gumption to face insurmountable odds and take bold decisions, which is synonymous with a person of flexible disposition.

In 1996, Dana enrolled into Northwestern University as a 'Speech Pathology' major. The university hosted the top program in the country. Three months into her coursework, it was clear that she and Speech Pathology was not a match and a change was needed.

The following summer, she headed to Verona, Italy, for a six-week Northwestern 'summer abroad' programme, where she studied Italian opera. Strange are the ways of destiny. It portends your future. It can take you to another location only to change the direction of your life.

In Verona, one of her classmates spoke about his major, Communications Studies. Each class he described piqued her interest and within hours of her return to the United States, she sent a request to the dean for a change of major. This proved to be her second career lesson—*when a window opens up to an opportunity and it feels right in your gut, seize the opportunity*. And you can do so only if you are flexible.

Upon graduation in 2000, Dana secured a position at a well-established promotional marketing agency. In her role, she served as an assistant account executive consulting to a Fortune 500 retailer.

The agency was small, allowing her to garner exposure and unique learning experiences with top level clients. While the work was interesting and fulfilling, poor management made the job unbearable. Dana's supervisor rose quickly in her career, without looking out for Dana. When in doubt, she panicked. If a client asked a question, instead of responding, 'Let me look into to the matter and get an answer,' she would scream at her staff for answers with hyperbolic urgency.

Dana opines, "Panic is a cancer than can disease a workplace. It makes work oppressive and if your employees fear sharing ideas, issues or problems, then it is unlikely that unique solutions will be introduced." It was here that Dana received some great advice from a more established colleague, "You will know when you are ready to leave a job."

In a few months' time, Dana knew with complete conviction, she was ready to move on. Though the job was less than ideal, she wouldn't have done it any differently because she learned a lot about herself, what she was willing to accept from an employer, and what kind of manager she would like to be when the time came.

In the fall of 2001, she joined a bigger promotional marketing agency, working with some of the top consumer packaged goods companies in the country. While she enjoyed the palpable energy of agency-life, she couldn't help but feel that no matter what great ideas her team came up with, the ultimate decision would rest in the hands of their clients. With that realization, she knew it was time to make the switch to the client side of marketing so that she could establish and drive the strategy for a brand. To facilitate her change, she enrolled into Northwestern University's Integrated Marketing Communications Masters program.

Upon graduation in 2005, she was hired as an Associate Marketing Manager by Rand McNally, *the iconic American brand for maps and road travel*. Originally hired to lead her team's Public Relations and Market Research efforts, her job description changed several times, reminding her of her first important career lesson—be flexible. She knew that a supervisor doesn't want to deal with opposition at every turn. All she did was to try as best as possible to embrace change with an adaptable and positive attitude. After a promotion to Marketing Manager, Dana was tasked with launching the company's first foray into toys—a line of games and activities that bring families together in the car.

An interesting concept and a great responsibility for an accomplished woman who knows that it is her flexible mindset that helps her evolve even during uncertain times. Dana says, "Given the uncertain economic times, it is more critical than ever to be flexible, don't panic, and try to see the positive in a situation."

Adaptability starts with flexibility and then breeds continual change. In the 21st century, even if an iota of rigidity sets into today's genius or visionary, he or she can become the victim of their own inflexibility tomorrow. You have to watch your mind and be open to all possibilities. You have to be prepared to take an immediate U-turn and change direction. You have to be prepared to attain the shape of water that changes its form with the type of vessel it floats in and out of, and yet it retains its quality to quench thirst. Therein lies the key to its adaptability. The window of opportunity does not open up every day and flexible people as Dana are ready to grasp it. To ring the changes wear the shoe of suppleness and bear in mind that true dominance comes from unconventional attitude, agility and flexibility.

***

9. Adjusting to Virtual and Cross-Cultural Communications.

Life, work and careers in 2025 will be largely virtual, and driven by video based communications. Technology has made it possible to connect people across the globe within a few minutes, and transcended differences in day and night, and miles and kilometres.

If you cannot attend your brother's wedding because you are miles away in another country or owing to factors beyond your control, you can still watch the wedding live. If you run the risk of missing your friend's bachelor party because of the traffic on the road, your laptop or smart phone can wire you up and zoom in to the party, where you can see it all. We are not too far away when we will be having a 'virtual conversation' with family, friends and strangers as we all tune in to watch the finals of the men's or women's tennis match at the Olympics. This will dramatically alter social behaviour and cultural dynamics.

As we witness the power of physical presence give way to the power of virtual communications, and 'face-to-face' meetings reduce, while virtual meetings gain acceptance across the globe, the power of the spoken and written word in an online and cross-cultural transnational world will matter more than ever before.

We live in an age where short emails, terse memos, cellphone notes, personal blogs, text messages, podcast, webinars and social media are being extensively used as communication vehicles. This will create the demand for engaging and creative communicators who can transcend cultural and national barriers, develop a unique communiqué for adoption of an ingenious idea, and devise a crisis communications plan that appeals to concerned stakeholders.

Monica Marie Sanchez-Weglicki graduated from college (bachelor's degree) and began a career in advertising and marketing, albeit she had aspired to be an artist and writer. After acquiring a master's degree in Integrated Marketing Communications from Northwestern University, she worked for OfficeMax (one of the largest office supplies retailer in the USA) in the field of Communications. Happily, communications fulfilled both needs of the artist and writer.

Her work experience spanning nine years, includes the fields of marketing, advertising and communications in homebuilding, medical, pharmaceutical, office supplies, online, advertising, retail, and corporate environments. In the U.S., Monica has lived in the city and countryside, and is now based overseas.

Monica's unique experiences are always worth going a mile to listen to. However, her one comment that intrigued me and that can be a great learning for every young mind was, "The world is interspersed with diverse cultures and work styles, and as young minds we are more likely than ever before, to work across divergent societies, nations, and cultures, in a pervasive online and mobile world, where the concept of time and distance has a new meaning. This would call for the development of an engaging and creative communications approach."

I requested Monica to suggest a few tips for a virtual based cross-cultural and technology driven world. Her advice is:

1. **Listen and really understand prior to making a comment or suggestion**

Rapid technological developments have created short, quick and differing communications styles best comprehended by listening first. While the world has become a smaller place, the local ethos of each location may be different and speak a particular language. When you listen first, you are setting up yourself to be a better verbal communicator. This may mean sacrifices and patience. You may respond with alacrity, but your colleague in another location may not be as quick to respond. You may have to help them come to it. And this can come easily if you remember to listen first. A good oral communicator knows this cardinal truth.

2. Whether it is age, gender or race, leave your cultural perceptions at the door

No one likes to admit to having them. But they do exist. Sometimes they are hidden in how we think we would do things versus the way another does something. The only way to conquer them is to face them and choose to grow.

a. My husband worked in Mergers and Acquisitions, which meant moving to new locations every few years. I adapted from city to countryside, as did our sprouting family. And as I adapted, I learnt that even individuals in high places (in companies) can carry prejudices or say rude things against cultures, and even I confronted some I thought I did not have. It is better to let them role off your back than to create an enemy. Leave the beast in its den if it is not your beast. The laws and good people in the working environments will protect you. It may sound too good to be true, but they came out of the woodwork for me.

3. Well-rounded written communicator

When it came to written communications, I used to be able to speak best from a creative standpoint. This was my strongpoint until my mentor, Carter Knox, put me in Human Resources communications. There I was introduced to corporate writing and allied topics. The human resources manual, reorganizations and other challenging pieces came to my desk on a daily basis. At times I had little over an hour to develop a piece. However, Carter had a plan. He was creating a well-rounded writer. From my experiences, I was able to become an even better creative writer. Now I could write within a framework.

Here are a few tips to help you on your way:

a. **Spice it up!** Whatever you are writing, make it interesting. We live in an era where people are reading less and less. That means you have less time to get their attention. That also demands more of you as a writer.

b. **Say more with fewer words.** An eloquent communicator can inspire with fewer words—after all less is more and short is sweet. Remember, heavy text can bore your reader and eliminate your readership. The last thing you want to do is destroy your last success.

c. **Consider your vehicle.** Are they reading this online in a magazine or intranet? Or it is a poster for a wall? What is the distance that they are reading it from? Larger distances mean less words and more punch. Small distances allow more freedom.

d. **Get technical.** Use a tracking or measurement tool. That way, you'll know what articles they click on in an online format. They are a variety of inexpensive tools. Add some tweaking and you can put a little science to help you improve your articles and communications.

***

Picture life in 2025... internet as a source of news and information may sound the death knell of newspapers. Intelligent cars would automatically navigate street lights and traffic, and obviate the need for you to be behind the wheels. Biometric chips (perhaps embedded in your body) or smart cards would incorporate features as your identification, driving license, medical history, degree certificates, airline ticket, financials, club membership, loyalty schemes and home entry access key. Printed books may give way to audio, mobile and e-books. Digital cash may supplant currency notes. High school graduation may happen at twelve years of age, and India may get its first 35 year old prime minister.

Oliver Goldsmith had once said, 'Every absurdity has a champion to defend it.' And what may seem as ludicrous today for it prevent change, will happen tomorrow. *1995 happened 15 years ago and 2025 is 15 years away from 2010*. Map the socio-economic, cultural, political, legal, creative, business, environmental and technological changes between 1995 and 2010, and then envision and anticipate the future 15 years from now...2025 is not too far way and waiting to happen.

Remember, growth is the most important aspect in personal and professional life... everything else is secondary. Growth keeps your mind young and your presence treasured. And growth comes with recurrent learning and change. Work to become your own Chief Change Officer before 'change' makes you its Chief Victim Officer.

★★★

Chapter 2

Script Your Own Career Destiny in an Uncertain World

Chapter 2 Script Your Own **Career Destiny** in an Uncertain World

Job or Entrepreneurship: Amidst a Boom Prepare for the Gloom

"Job Security is gone. The driving force of a career must come from the individual."

—Homa Bahrami

"What's the good of being a genius if you can't use it as an excuse for being unemployed?"

—Gerald Barzan

10. Learn to Wear Unlike Hats—Job and Entrepreneurship

In 2007, when the Indian economy was booming and a compensation of ten million rupees for a senior young professional was seen as commonplace, I was addressing a small group of young executives in Bengaluru (The Silicon Valley of India). We had a lively discussion on jobs, entrepreneurship, compensation, education, creative avocations and networking. At the end of the discussion, an ex-colleague popped a pertinent question, "What do you think will be the most important aspect for Young Minds to bear in mind for the next 10-15 years?'

I smiled and replied, "I am no Nostradamus, astrologer, career counsellor or human resources czar, but my sixth sense tells me that each of us who will work for a minimum

I wonder which path should I tread—job or entrepreneurship?
Entrepreneurship
Job & Entrepreneurship
Job
Develop skills for both. Should a job not work out or you face a lay off, you should be able to transition into entrepreneurship and vice versa!

of two more decades must develop skills to wear unlike hats—job and entrepreneurship. That would be one of my key recommendations to young minds wanting to make a successful career in a small world. Go acquire skills to be successful in a job and your own business. Should the job not work out, you should be able to transition into entrepreneurship and should your business fold up, you should be able to get a suitable job."

My ex-colleague replied, 'I am not sure if I agree with you Pushpendra. Few are comfortable in both roles—job or entrepreneurship. Some value their independence, creative freedom and cannot work under anybody so they are not suited for jobs, while others prefer a secure existence under the aegis of a well established company and are cut out only for jobs. So why do you feel it is important to acquire skills for the duo - job and entrepreneurship?'

I responded, 'Because all over the world a number of well established companies may cease to exist by 2025 or be unable to create sufficient growth for large scale or extended periods of employment. Because today's domestic and international icons of economic prowess that post adequate profits on their home turf may report losses internationally or vice versa, requiring large scale pink slips or layoffs. Because, more than ever before, the threat of mergers and acquisitions is stalking senior and middle management at organizations worldwide. Because top management prefers layoffs, pink slips or pay cuts to trim costs. Because decisions taken by select top management executives, can adversely affect thousands of employees at home and overseas. Because greed at the top can destroy 75-100 year old venerated companies. Because for every one successful entrepreneur there are 100 failed entrepreneurship attempts. Because for every 100 innovative business ideas or business plans, only a few are successful to get the backing of an angel investor or venture capitalist. Because for every 100 creative pursuits only a handful get recognition, and because the cost and standard of living has increased and only a few are prepared to struggle, dig their heels in, or work unassumingly to live their dreams. Thus, my friend I believe that my fellow young legion should develop skills for the duo—job and entrepreneurship.'

The discussion did not come to a conclusive end. My ex-colleague is right about people being more suited for one of the two—job or entrepreneurship.

While I agree with her basic premise about the aforesaid suitability factor and appropriate fit, I beg to differ a little: In a competitive world where only a small percentage of the total population and their family have the luxury of living their dreams with or without struggles, and the rest of the world are saddled with a relentless objective—to feed, educate and provide for their family, siblings or kids, we the young need to adapt faster and equip ourselves for all possibilities in a globally connected and dynamic world. When confronted with uncertain and difficult times, we may have to redeploy our skills for a better future.

I am not suggesting for a minute that you should not live your bold dreams, pursue the 'right fit' career option, take risks, follow the unconventional route or be prepared to struggle or fail in your path to greatness. I am all for walking on uncharted paths. Yet, I merely wish to convey that when economic insecurity shrouds our lives (and should you wish to), role changes only shape up the experiences and lessons of life, and if the essence of a job or entrepreneurship is to be a 'service, food, shelter, clothing, education, recognition, identity, career, joy and smile provider' then you can make a difference in either of the roles (job or entrepreneurship) by grooming yourself for all eventualities.

Should the need arise and a prolonged economic necessity warrant a necessary role change (the economic meltdown of 2008-09 is not the last financial crisis we will witness in our life time), you will be prepared to walk successfully in the moccasins of an entrepreneur or a salaried professional.

The years 2008 and 2009 will serve as great lessons for us should we want to profit from the global economic crisis or financial carnage. The international economic decline and the subsequent global slowdown have meant loss of millions of jobs across the world, even as unemployment rates are disturbing to the mind.

Most economists have gone wrong. The best of global leadership has been caught unprepared for a contraction of such magnitude. And as individuals, we are left to the mercy of the consequences of strategic missteps pursued by decision makers at certain iconic organizations. The power of a powerful minority cannot be condoned—the choices and decisions of a few, have affected the lives of millions. Everything is integrated, they say. Welcome to a 'small' world.

The manufacturing, agricultural, trading and service sectors are inter-related as couples in a relationship or marriage. When one slows down, the other gets affected. It is a chain which connects all—unemployed, mainstream or non-mainstream professional.

Thus, if there is one imperative professional lesson to draw from any economic wreckage or periods of uncertainty, it is to take destiny in your hands and if required be prepared to wear different or unlike hats, transition to a suitable job should your entrepreneurial venture face rough weather (and you are not ready to stick it out) or create your own entrepreneurial (baby) project should you face a pink slip or layoff.

During tough economic times, you may be caught between the trepidation and the thrill of launching your maiden venture... why take undue risks, after all if you have been laid off, it is better to play safe and continue looking for another job. Remember, not all who get the pink slip will get a job very soon, and nobody but you will script your destiny.

You are advised to bear in mind that the best of innovations have been created during adversity and uncertain periods. You could be the next innovator or valuable job creator. In tough times, you could create something out of nothing, and as the business thrives it will give you the courage to create another venture. Then, in no measure will any future economic slowdown dampen your spirits or squash the hopes of hordes of young wannabe entrepreneurs waiting in the wings to act upon their instincts and emulate your story.

In a digital economy, you have cost-efficient alternatives. You can marshal cost effective technological solutions to unleash your online or mobile based business. And even if your business fails or does not reach the heights you envisaged, somebody smart will hire you to blaze a trail for his organization—that will be the emerging small world for you, where professionals will be more acceptable and tolerant of reversal of roles—job to entrepreneurship and vice versa. After all he who hires you cannot guarantee the security of his own job and may depend on you at some point in time for his survival or progress. Strange are the ways of the world.

***

11. A Month with the Underprivileged – Lessons For the Mainstream and Non-Mainstream Professional

In the new world order, you would first have to be a good social citizen to then be counted as a brilliant professional, creative czar or inspiring leader. This may sound fashionable and fairly easy to adopt, but when it comes to pragmatic execution, is fraught with challenges and uneasiness for most.

Those who can go through the out of comfort zone experience of making small beginnings as a good social citizen, can provide a far more rich and meaningful contribution by means of their chosen profession. I recommend, you use three weeks to a month of your vacation time, preferably while in college, university or during the early part of your professional career to volunteer or work full time for the benefit of the underprivileged through a non-profit organization (NGO), some other professional establishment or by yourself independently. Trust me, at the end of your cherished experience, you will stands out as a far more sensitive marketer, communicator, public servant or politician, an improved writer, painter, reporter or actor, and a better strategist, doctor, lawyer, engineer, number cruncher or analyst.

It is best to expose yourself to both sides of the coin - profit and non profit world - when in college, university or during the early part of your career, before you get submerged in the material trappings that dictate our lives. Even a small or marginal exposure to poverty, deprivation, philanthropy, hunger, slums, villages, struggles, and hope, can lead you to make a 'true' difference through your chosen avocation and play a creative role in shaping the destiny of future generations.

In August 2007, I took a calculated risk to move from consulting for the 'Top of the Pyramid' (the rich) to the 'Bottom of the Pyramid' (the poorest socio-economic group). A shift to the 'microfinance' (financial services for the poor or low income people that primarily encompasses savings, loans/ credit, insurance, and funds transfer services) domain was a logical corollary and an opportunity for me to experience life at the 'base of the pyramid.' I was sincere in my attempt and wanted to understand the mindset of the underprivileged to help them work their way out of poverty with dignity and pride. God bestowed me a favour and I was offered a job by ACCION International (Headquartered in Boston, USA). Unknown to most in a small world, ACCION has helped build and strengthen some of the most successful microfinance institutions in the world through sustainable solutions to poverty alleviation.

In December 2005, the Bill & Melinda Gates Foundation had granted $5.8 million to ACCION International for usage in ACCION's microfinance programmes for the poor in India and West Africa. In January 2002, ACCION was one of the 11 charities worldwide accredited by the World Economic Forum's Global Exchange for Social Investment. ACCION had played a vital role in creating economic and social change and I was excited to be a part of this wonderful opportunity that would abet my personal social responsibility goals. I was seconded to the ACCION-YES (Bank) MICROFINANCE India (YES MFI) venture based out of Mumbai.

Before my move to Mumbai, I was sent by ACCION to undergo rigorous microfinance training being conducted in Lima, Peru. The orientation training programme was being conducted for new employees who had joined ACCION from various parts of the world—US, Canada, Latin America, Africa, India, and Philippines. The holistic training was a great mix of spirited classroom sessions and a few 'day long' field trips to lower income areas in Lima.

'Impressive' is an understatement for the dogged character displayed by the people of the low income and poor areas of Lima. What we observed was a true marvel. Lima's 'bottom of the pyramid' presented an inspiring story of how 'hard work, persistence, hope and entrepreneurship spirit of the underprivileged coalesced with ACCION's proven consulting methodology and Mibanco's (a leading microfinance bank in Lima) business acumen, adroit risk management (including use of credit scoring and credit bureau) practices, unique marketing, sales promotion and communications efforts, and array of financial products and services (savings, loans/credit, insurance, funds transfer, cell phone and ATM technology), had alleviated poverty for many and created lakhs of micro-entrepreneurs (majority of them are women) from scratch. As partners, ACCION and Mibanco have been instrumental in the development of a very advanced microfinance business in Peru, possibly among the best in the world.

Upon my return to Mumbai, I took it upon myself to spend a considerable time in the slums and low income areas of Mumbai, as I was responsible for the marketing and product development of the YES MFI venture. You learn marketing, product development and communications by regular field visits, current and prospective customer feedback, speaking with customers in their language, and a survey of living and working conditions of the underprivileged. I had to forget all the latest marketing and communications practices, I had acquired a few years ago in US—once again the time had come to unlearn and relearn.

Albeit, I spent a very short period with ACCION and was credited with giving the microfinance venture (in Mumbai) its official name - 'Sampann' (translates into prosperity, growth and well being in Hindi), all I did to arrive at a suitable name was to obtain the feedback of prospective and current customers spanning different communities on what they felt would be the most appropriate name for a microfinance initiative in a city of vastly contrasting fortunes.

One of the most important aspects of marketing and branding is to get the name of an outfit to strike a chord with its customers. Sampann to my mind reflects the microfinance ethos and vision that ACCION hope to achieve.

The underprivileged intelligent folk in various parts of Mumbai had taught me a great lesson in marketing—hear and listen to the voice of the customer on the street. They had taught me that even with very little material comforts the voiceless had big hearts and can think big. They had taught me that entrepreneurs are made to live and fight risks each day. They had taught me the importance of customized communications, and they had opened my eyes to a range of business ventures that operate out of diverse low income areas and slums—that there are limitless options to explore as an entrepreneur.

You can well imagine how fortunate I am to have been blessed with unforgettable experiences that came out of my interactions with the underprivileged (yet intelligent, witty, street smart, giving and mentally tough) in Mumbai.

A small 'personal social responsibility goal' and an 'out of the comfort zone' career move termed as suicidal by some of my friends and colleagues in the consultancy and services industry, provided me lessons big enough to last a lifetime. The icing on the cake: through the venture, I met some amazing people who have become special friends.

***

12. Turn Over a New Leaf—Master the Art of Negotiations

Never before has the 'art of successful negotiations' been as pertinent as today. If you wish to be a top notch employer or employee, or wish to skilfully juggle between a job and self employment, nothing will be quite as important as mastering the art of deft negotiations.

In the autumn of 2005, I met Professor Fred Crandall for the first time. I had heard a lot about his negotiations expertise and the extraordinary 'negotiations' course he taught each quarter at the IMC programme at Northwestern University. Dr. Fred Crandall is a senior member of Watson Wyatt's (a reputed global consulting firm focused on human capital and financial management) office in Chicago. He has worked with organizations in a wide range of industries as financial services, manufacturing, distribution and logistics, retail and wholesale trade, route sales and service, health care, hi-tech and utilities. Dr. Crandall had also served as national partner at PricewaterhouseCoopers, and is an alumnus of UCLA, University of California at Berkeley, and University of Minnesota. With amazing credentials as above, I thought it imperative to enrol for the quarter long 'negotiations' course taught by Dr. Fred Crandall.

It was early days in the course. I was looking for a flash of brilliance from the intelligent man. He did not disappoint me and put a million dollar question to the 40 of us (select classmates and I) who had enrolled for the 'negotiations' course. He asked us if we thought 'Everything is negotiable' 'That is a simple question with a simple answer,' so I felt.

The class was rather vocal and a number of divergent opinions came out as the discussion progressed. The answers may have been right, but required deeper introspection and one precisely understood then, why negotiations is an art and science, and a fascinating discipline. The class was an amalgam of accomplished, intelligent, fun loving, versatile

Let me initially offer $750,000 to buy his company. At best, he will ask for $850,000. That would still be an attractive buy!
Let me ask for $1million for the sale of my company. **Post-negotiations**, even if I get $850,000—I'll be pleased!!!

and competitive classmates from the East and West, who had worked across services, manufacturing and trading sector, including public service. Subsequently, we were involved in wide-ranging negotiations assignments and exercises for the quarter long course, encompassing domestic and international negotiations for personal and professional growth.

We had to record the progress we made as negotiators each week and to my delight the positive difference in my negotiating style was tangible. The course was a great blend of academic theory and pragmatic application of negotiations for success in almost all walks of life. It was one of the most interesting and intellectually stimulating courses of my academic sojourn at Northwestern University. Manipulative, absurd or unbelievable as it may sound, I was convinced by the end of the quarter that 'Everything is negotiable.'

Over the last three years, each time I have got into a professional negotiations exercise (within India or overseas) with the belief that 'Everything is negotiable,' it has worked for me. I am pretty certain not all my classmates would agree with the aforesaid statement and a number of you may have your doubts too, but I exhort you to read on and decide for yourself. I owe my ascent as a better negotiator to Dr. Fred Crandall. He is a brilliant negotiator—an absolute genius. He takes 'negotiations as an art and science' to new heights, and crafts his protégé to win the negotiations process in a way that is beneficial to all parties concerned.

We seldom realize but negotiations are a part of our everyday life—with our beloved, family, friends, colleagues, associates and acquaintances. We negotiate and so does the person we communicate with negotiate. When we buy a car we negotiate, when we buy a house we negotiate, when we move jobs we negotiate, when we pursue a business deal we negotiate, when we are dating we negotiate, when we want a raise in pocket money from our parent we negotiate, when we communicate with kids we negotiate, when we buy a computer we negotiate, when we get a cellphone we negotiate, when we want a promotion we negotiate, when we want to save a job we negotiate, when we want capital for our new or existing business we negotiate, when we want to lease an office or residential premises we negotiate, when our manuscript is ready for printing we negotiate, when our painting is ready for exhibition we negotiate, and when we want something badly or at any cost we negotiate. Negotiations is not merely about saving money or asking for more. It is not about one-upmanship. It is a process of using a wide variety of skills to create a valuable proposition for all concerned.

The small world has created outstanding negotiators in all spheres of life—public and private enterprise. Observe a supplier and a retailer negotiate. Watch a car dealer negotiate with a prospective customer. Witness the negotiations between domestic staff and the lady of the house. Catch the sight of a CEO negotiating a bonus with the board of directors. See how an author negotiates an increase in royalty with the publisher, and witness a photographer negotiating his price with a client. All these examples will help you hone your negotiating skills. In a small world, you will find walking dictionaries and examples of adroit negotiators with or without formal or higher education. You can learn the art of negotiations from them.

Alternatively, you can read up books, articles, blogs and newsletters on negotiations, and then start negotiating (using a trial and error approach) on 'small' personal and professional matters, and develop your own negotiations style. You will make mistakes, but mistakes will make you a better negotiator. You can also enrol in for a short course or training programme on negotiations, which will provide you the necessary tools and techniques to skilfully negotiate pressing matters that govern your personal and professional life. Remember, the important thing is to formalize negotiations and give it a suitable framework that includes concrete, specific and measurable objectives, alternatives and an astute strategy.

The difference between a good, average and bad negotiator rests on the importance accorded to the basic premise 'Is everything negotiable?' Try two scenarios and go into separate negotiations with a different mindset—first 'Yes everything is negotiable' and second 'Some things are not negotiable.' I am not asking you to compromise with your beliefs, but within accepted ethical behaviour, try the aforesaid approaches and observe the results. You will be surprised how the former approach will work for you nine out of ten times should you negotiate keeping in mind a 'mutual benefit' set-up or 'win-win situation' for parties to a negotiation. Start negotiating today. Negotiate small or big, negotiate in college or in university, negotiate at home or at work, negotiate overseas or within the confines of the country, but start today.

Whether you are in the creative or analytical profession, whether you work for a profit or non profit entity, whether you are a student or have just graduated, whether you are without a job or are about to shut shop as self-employed, and whether you are gainfully employed or are a successful entrepreneur, it is imperative for you to continually hone the art of negotiations.

The journey from 2010 to 2025 may include success and failures, fame and ignominy, profit and loss, the memorable and the unforgettable, but chiselling and polishing the art of negotiations will keep you saleable and razor-sharp to ride over adverse or moderate circumstances that arise out of factors beyond your control or not of your making.

***

13. Tomorrow's CEO Will Come From HR and PR—Develop Your HR & PR Skills

Prior to my academic sojourn at Northwestern University, I served dual roles at CCMC. In addition to being a consultant on marketing and sales with a focus on bank cards and personal finance, I was responsible for the public relations function that included media management and external communications. CCMC and I were accorded regular media

Tomorrow's CEOs will come from which discipline—finance, marketing or IT?
People (HR) make iconic companies and 'Perception' (PR) makes them credible. Tomorrow's CEO's will come from HR & PR disciplines.

coverage by prominent publications in India, namely *The Economic Times, The Times of India, The Financial Express, Business Standard, and Business Today*.

In the year 2000, *The Wall Street Journal*, New York, quoted CCMC in a story that appeared on the first page. This was brought to our notice by a reputed business journalist in Mumbai. And what followed was more visibility with the media and increase in the client roster. I was responsible for CCMC's mention in *The Wall Street Journal* (happened again in 2004), primarily because I followed a simple dictum—use Public Relations (PR) to build a brand.

Yet the credit for making me a far more holistic and cost effective marketer goes to Dr. Patricia T. Whalen because I attended her incredible 'Public Relations: Strategies and Tactics' class at Medill School, Northwestern University, during the winter quarter of early 2005. Prior to her academic career, Dr. Whalen spent nearly 20 years in corporate marketing and communications positions. She served as the top corporate communication executive for Clark Equipment Company, a Fortune 300 automotive manufacturing firm that is now part of Ingersoll-Rand and Eaton Corporations.

Dr. Whalen also served for eight years as Director of Marketing and Communication for Comsat Corporation, a Washington D.C. based international telecommunications firm that was subsequently acquired by the Lockheed-Martin Corporation. While at Comsat, she received the chairman's award as the firm's most productive manager and helped her division achieve the title, 'Telecom Marketing Department of the Year' from *Sales & Marketing Management Magazine*.

Professor Patricia Whalen's class was rather participatory, even as she went out of her way to encourage domestic and international students to share their thoughts and experiences. She wanted us to learn from each other. What ensued was exchange of interesting PR occurrences and episodes that encompassed US and international work arenas. To my mind, Dr. Whalen's endeavour was to provide us an understanding of discerning public relations practices that would enable us to better integrate PR with allied functions within an organization, namely marketing, finance, human resources, among others.

The benefit of being taught PR from a multitalented individual who had been an acclaimed marketing and public relations professional and now a top notch academic meant the best of real world training and academic guidance encompassing PR strategic planning and research, media relations, corporate communications, crisis communications, PR measurement and evaluation, internal branding and employee communications.

Since the completion of the public relations course, I have formulated holistic and cost effective PR plans, crisis communications and media relations strategies for reputed clients in India and overseas... and yes, they have been implemented too.

Thanks to Dr. Whalen my strength as a marketer improved because of the new found ability to integrate marketing with avant-garde public relations techniques. My professional acumen has been enhanced because of the sagacious skills acquired from her to communicate effectively with finance professionals, IT czars, advertising and branding gurus, human resources experts, and allied stakeholders.

Today I can wear multiple hats (New Age marketing and communications consultant, including author and writer) far more effectively, and communicate the importance of PR for tomorrow's mainstream and non-mainstream professional.

After eight years of teaching at the Medill IMC programme at Northwestern University, Dr. Whalen moved to DePaul University in Chicago, where she is an assistant professor and director of the graduate program in public relations and advertising in the College of Communication. She is the author of two books on marketing and public relations: *A Marketers Guide to Public Relations in the 21st Century (Thomson, 2006)*, co-authored with Thomas L. Harris; and *Corporate Communication From A To Z—An Encyclopedia for Public*

Relations & Marketing Professionals (IABC, 2005). I am glad I was at the right place at the right time to comprehend the imminent 'rise and march' of public relations towering over other important functions (marketing, finance, operations, engineering and information technology) in time to come.

I am often asked by college and university students, "Where will tomorrow's CEO come from?" As requirements vary between industries or business, it is difficult to make an accurate prediction. But if you were to ask me to hazard a guess or make an educated inference, my opinion will not impress most. I am in the minority. Most will say finance, marketing, engineering, production or information technology, but at the risk of being proven wrong, I put my money on Public Relations or Human Resources (HR). My inexplicable sixth sense tells me that by 2025, a number of big and medium sized companies will have CEOs from a PR or HR background.

With talent management, social responsibility, image management, ethics and corporate governance becoming increasingly important factors for stakeholders (including investors and customers) in an organization, I can envision a future where PR and HR will be *treated* at par with perhaps, two of the most important (widely regarded) present day functions of businesses– marketing and finance.

People make iconic companies and perception makes them credible. HR and PR epitomize these aspects better than any other management function. You can hire the experts i.e. the best CFO to create more wealth, the ablest CTO to develop the most innovative hi-tech solutions, and the smartest CMO to be the trailblazer for cutting-edge, innovative and customized products and services, but for an uncertain, evanescent and fast evolving world, you require a 'change manager and sagacious human capital specialist' as a CEO, which to my mind would be best provided by an HR specialist or expert.

In a competitive world where discerning individuals decide which organizations to work for based on its environmental friendly policies and customers buy from companies that have adopted social responsibility goals as a belief system, the public relations czar too would be a great choice for the CEO role.

It is a fallacy to continue to assume that marketing and finance people know best how to run companies. If this were true, why did the economic crisis of 2008-09 touted as the biggest financial wreckage in decades mar the fortunes of some of the most renowned or iconic companies across the world? Apparent reasons—greed and wrong decisions. Veneered reasons—Lack of visionary leadership and image management skills. Marketing may be my first child and public relations the second offspring, but at the cost of speaking out of turn or shooting myself in the foot, I do feel that future CEOs will come from public relations and human resources domain.

It is imperative to demolish stereotypes—'PR and HR is a soft skill or meant for the weaker sex.' PR cannot be defined merely as publicity and HR as hiring or recruitment managers. The major components of PR include media relations, investor relations, corporate social responsibility, image management, new media, internal branding and employee communications, crisis communications, issues management and speechwriting.

Human Resources go beyond recruitment and selection. It includes, among others, organizational development and leadership, diversity, talent management, training and development, career customization, succession planning, employee appraisals, change management, international HR, and compensation and benefits.

I would exhort, every young mind to spend adequate time understanding the nuances of public relations and human resources. Whether you work in the mainstream or non mainstream realm, you will need public relations and human resources skills at some point in time. Irrespective of whether you take the self-employment or the salaried employee route, you will need new age PR and HR skills to build your own brand, your organization's profile, and augment the development of your establishment's human capital.

Young Minds, HR and PR are getting hotter by the day. You are requested to remember a cardinal principle—You cannot create an iconic brand without strategic PR nor can you create a great organization without adept HR. Please remember this equation:

Numero Uno People + Numero Uno Public Perception = Numero Uno Organization.

***

14. Small is Vital and Magic—Go Experience it

Small is vital. For years we have been led to believe that a job with big companies, international corporations and global conglomerates is perhaps, the best career option, an easy route to asset creation and big ticket consumer loans, the safety net for a protracted successful career, and the strategic direction to a 'great catch' status with the opposite sex. My father worked for a foreign bank for over three decades, which exposed me to great minds in the country and overseas. And yet he told me that it is a fallacy to think that the best leaders and managers work only for large companies or renowned entrepreneurs.

Careers with big companies make you a subject matter expert, expose you to cutting-edge management, leadership and technology practices, provide high visibility, create a global mindset and an international network, and offer attractive compensation packages (works rather well for the family). It has its tremendous advantages. But in the 21st century, few large corporations can provide you job security, flat organizational structure, cross-functional work opportunities, and entrepreneurship skills.

In the new age order, you have to look out for yourself. In a cut-throat world replete with regular layoffs, pink slips, and curtailed benefits, the concept of 'job security,' the mainstay of the big corporation in the last century is passé. If you are not assured of a lifelong job, you must at least have some modicum of surety.

Self employment would give you that self-dependency and control feeling. Going small (without giving up on your big dreams) would perhaps, be the most effective conduit to keep the reins of your life in your hands and become an excellent breeding ground for possible entrepreneurship. Welcome to the world of small enterprises.

Globally, some of the finest minds in diverse businesses are employed with small enterprises. Small companies excel at creating entrepreneurs and provide greater opportunities for regular interaction with top management. Such companies may be less glamorous, but they can expose you a lot faster to different roles thereby sowing the seeds of entrepreneurship better than large companies.

Small enterprises are a great training ground for wide-ranging skills, cross-functional included. Necessary skills required to turn into an 'overnight or urgently mandated' entrepreneur can also be best acquired with a small company. Consider the options—operate a photocopy machine, design and manage a website, understand production, legal, financial, human resources, technology and investor management issues, copy write an advertisement, develop a press release for media coverage, create 'new media' plans, polish customer service and telephone skills, make a sales pitch, formulate marketing strategies, interact closely with subject matter experts or gain direct access to senior management, work on statistical software, conduct market research and write reports—you can learn it all.

It would be a great idea to spend a few years with a small company. If not, then I would implore you to spend a quarter or summer as an 'intern or a resident' with a small company or a start-up. You will acquire 'rich and valuable experience,' be able to 'explore your interests or tap your innate or latent potential' before you decide on a career path, and get an opportunity early on in your career to pick on the collective brains of top management, which is a rarity at a large company.

I have been fortunate to have been exposed to the small, medium and the big within India and overseas. I have learnt the art of fast and creative new product development from the small. I have honed my cross-functional skills with the small. I have learnt to take quick decisions from the small. I have learnt to take risks from the small. I have learnt to share laurels from the small. I have learnt to operate statistical software from the small. I have learnt how to manage media relations and new media from the small. I have learnt important aspects of online fraud prevention from the small. I have learnt the art of financial prudence from the small. I have learnt the art of caring for your colleagues from the small. I have enhanced my creativity with the small. I have improved as a writer and communicator because of the small. I have developed new business models because of the cerebral depth of the top management at the small. I have learnt to be proud of doing my own photocopy and preparing my own tea... from the small. Small is vital and small is magic. Go experience it.

***

15. Your Voice and Speech—Perk up Force or Permanent Wound

When the affable Amit Kakri of the Mumbai based, National Ideological Movement for Better Literature and Education (NIMBLE) foundation quizzed me about the importance of 'voice and speech' and apprised me about its significance in shaping the development of young minds in an emerging virtual 'voice and speech' driven culture, I thought it best to note our conversation and present them in the book.

Pay special attention to the often condoned aspect of 'effective speech and tone of voice' in shaping professional success on a job or as an entrepreneur.

Amit asked, "How often do we recognize that our speech is the most important part of our personality? How often do we realize that there is an uneasy air mounting between two professionals, colleagues or associates, not because one has used offensive words at the other, but simply because the tone of the voice was unacceptable?"

"You make a very good point," I said.

Amit continued, "Even if we do realize the importance of voice and speech, most of us are not even aware how sound is produced by the human body and how words are created?

"The importance of voice and speech in human life cannot be exaggerated. In fact speech alone is responsible for building human relations. For instance, while speaking a sentence, by just changing the emphasis from one word to another, the meaning changes. Likewise, in a particular sentence, if one was to move from one pause to another the meaning could change, sometimes rather drastically.

"The impact of the message you want to communicate depends only 10 percent on the words used. The voice controls the balance 90 percent. The tone says something about your honesty, commitment and enthusiasm. Often relations are marred not because of offensive language used, but because the tone was abrasive or impolite."

I asked, "In your estimation where does clarity in speech figure?"

Amit replied, "Clarity in speech is another area of consequence. Quite often there is a tendency to rush through with the communication without pronouncing each syllable clearly. Again improper or inadequate use of modulation, pause, range of pitch, among other factors, can result in speech becoming unintelligible and dreary."

"How do you rate the present scenario with speech and voice skills?" I inquired.

"Unfortunately, we find the present state on speech and speaking skills rather dismal. Many university graduates cannot express themselves clearly and efficiently. Often they are not even sure of what they want to convey. There is no proper use of modulation, pause, or range of pitch; as a result the speech is incoherent and uninteresting. Communications is a mirror of the personality of an individual. As the youth of the small world, embarks into their chosen professions, good voice and clear speech will provide them a tremendous head start."

The subject of voice has now come into focus mainly due to the efforts of voice trainers and speech experts like Mr. Satish Kakri and Mr. Amit Kakri of NIMBLE Foundation. In the words of Mr. Satish Kakri, "Speech is perhaps the single most significant aspect of a personality and determines to a large extent one's standing in society. We must remember each individual uses his voice from the time he wakes up in the morning till he retires to bed."

NIMBLE Foundation has taken on the onus for training students, faculty and professionals in voice and speech, and has been conducting programmes for the last five years on 'Voice Culture and Speaking Skills' in Mumbai. Amit apprised me that the popular 15-session programme covers all aspects of voice enhancement, including voice modulation, overcoming common speaking defects, breath control and exercises for the pitch, tone and level of voice.

My discussion with Amit took me back to professional instances where I have witnessed the best of ideas not being accepted merely because of the tone of voice or the easy acceptance of contradictory opinion because of the tone in which it was conveyed. I have been a spectator to contrasting professional scenarios—the 'voice in tongue' being used as a sharp and sarcastic weapon for professional self aggrandizement and the 'voice in tongue' being used to inspire and motivate colleagues for enhanced team work. And I have observed smart professionals win tiresome arguments not because of their analytical skills, but by their tone and speaking skills.

It is imperative to harness our voice and speech skills, because as a vital element of communications excellence, these will allow us to gain an upper hand amidst an emerging virtual 'voice and speech' driven world. In tomorrow's world the master of voice and speech will reach the heart and soul of people, move them, inspire them, motivate them, and lead them. The clock is ticking... call your voice trainer and speech expert today. If the body needs a personal or physical trainer, the impending virtual world needs a session with the voice and speech coach. Remember your voice and speech can either be a perk up force or create a permanent wound for those around you.

***

16. International Business—The Propeller to Survive in a Spaghetti World

In the autumn of 2005, I underwent a course on 'International Business Strategy.' The course was being taught by Professor Daniel F. Spulber, Elinor Hobbs Distinguished Professor of International Business and Professor of Management Strategy at the Kellogg School of Management, Northwestern University. Prof. Spulber is the founder of Kellogg's International Business & Markets Programme. He is the author of twelve books and the founding editor of the *Journal of Economics & Management Strategy*.

You can well imagine how fortunate and blessed I was to be a part of the renowned professor's 'International Business Strategy' class.

Because of the passion and expertise Prof. Spulber brought to the subject, now and again, over coffee breaks, I would pick on his brains to enhance my understanding of the dynamics of global business. He was very patient with my inquisitions and his perspicacity on 'international business' in the context of international retail, transnational manufacturing, and global services sector was truly exceptional.

What was most impressive was the in-depth knowledge he possessed about social, cultural, economic and business practices spanning continents and countries that grace our universe, particularly nations that come up seldom for discussions.

The hallmark of an outstanding professor lies in his or her ability to get the class to participate in intelligent and lively discussions. The virtuoso that he is at bringing out 'participatory and spirited deliberations,' he made his eclectic class learn more from each other than mere manuals or text book. He dwarfed his attainments to make his students feel very comfortable in his presence.

Among other aspects, what amazed me was his comprehension of emerging countries, particularly India and China. His predilection for observing trends in emerging countries that go unnoticed, his recommendation to students to work and travel internationally (particularly in India and China), and his brilliance in observing unique and veneered strengths of different cultures make him truly an outstanding professor of international business strategy and an extraordinary conversationalist.

Before my academic sojourn at Northwestern University, I had been part of international consulting assignments, but it is Prof. Spulber who taught me the importance of *'strategic internationalization'* of one's avocation, business, passion or interests—be it a salaried professional or an entrepreneur, an actor or reporter, architect or writer, consumer activist or environmentalist, professor or student. To successfully do so, I would advocate and implore every young mind (non-business and business background) to attend a course on 'international business.' International business does not connote only competitive strategies, foreign direct investment, economic analysis, market entry, exports or imports. It goes beyond to include an understanding of divergent cultures, their areas of expertise or specialization, and the unique aspects of its products and services. In a small world it makes you think innovation and attain big.

The urge to move beyond the domestic or home turf will be important to survive in a spaghetti world, where things change as fast as you slurp the noodles in your mouth. In a digital and knowledge based world, understanding of international business may prove to be your shield or security cover during tough times. When the chips are down and mere survival comes into question, knowledge of 'international business' can be your propeller to connect with somebody within your area of interest across the world and start afresh.

Even with basic knowledge of 'international business' practices, new ventures and unexplored options will open up. Young Minds, you could create jobs and generate large scale employment if exposure to international business perspectives can be attained when young and at your prime. Remember, 'International attainments overshadow domestic stardom' (A quote from my first book *"Win the Battles of Life & Relationships"*). You too could go international with your occupation, interests, commitments and network. And exposure to international business will just make it easier.

***

17. All Roads will lead to a Business Plan–The Next Milestone

Envisage a scenario—You are disgruntled with your job, have been laid off or wish to be your own boss. You have a few options. One of them is to step into the world of 'freedom' or entrepreneurship. You have a great idea (perhaps the resources too) and cannot wait to get started.

Alternatively, you may be in a conundrum on how to get the venture organized (only a great idea, but little or no resources) and going. *Not to worry... all roads lead to an important document termed as 'business plan.'* On most instances (exceptions apart), a business plan is the first step you take to put your thoughts and dreams together within a framework. You commence your entrepreneurship journey by writing your business plan. 15-20 pages will suffice. At the end of the plan you will be sparkling with clarity of thought and a road map of how to live your dream through your own venture.

In a small world, it is great to see young minds taking the entrepreneurial route through a creative, proven, innovative or differentiating idea. A number of young MBAs acquire the requisite knowledge and skills to develop a comprehensive 'business plan' while pursuing their management education or when employed. However, a large section of young business graduates or non-business graduates struggle to create a well thought out business plan—because they do not know how to do so or think of a business plan as a daunting exercise. On the contrary it is not a difficult exercise, and software, resources and books galore on the subject (online and offline) provide step by step direction to create a discerning business plan.

You could also enrol in for a short course on 'developing a business plan' or get assistance from your friends, family, colleagues or associates who have dabbled with business plans or can advice you on how to develop one. The goal is to create a cost effective, adaptable, well researched and holistic plan within a specified time frame (usually 4-12 weeks) that can get you into the execution mode soon after and rechristen you as 'Founder & CEO' of your new venture.

While a business plan may not guarantee success as an entrepreneur or be a mandatory document (especially, if you have loads of money to start a business), it provides a strategic framework and direction for an entrepreneurial venture. A sound business plan will not supplant execution skills required to take the business to greater heights, but it will abet clarity of thought to get the stakeholders of an organization on the same page.

A business plan is an important document for all types of organizations—existing or starts ups (creative ventures, profit and nonprofits). Were you to ever head a division with a big domestic or international company, you will be required to present a business plan to your superiors. If you were to start your own venture, you will need to develop a business plan to receive funding from banks, angel investors, venture capitalists or private equity players.

Make sure you know how to write a business plan... with a caveat, should you take the entrepreneurship route, please do not 'outsource' your business plan i.e. do not request or hire a friend, consultant, family member, professor, colleague or associate to write or create your business plan. Your dream requires your hard work, thoughts and direction, so write or create your own business plan, because only you can best convince others of your great idea or communicate or defend your thought process coherently. If you are not the person working on the plan. at the opportune moment you will find it difficult to convince other stakeholders or perhaps, execute effectively on the vision propounded by you.

***

18. Do You Have an Elevator Speech?

Do you have an elevator speech (or elevator pitch)? Can you explain your idea, profile, talent, business, project, product, service or specialization in 30 seconds (the average time span of an elevator ride from the first floor to the top floor or vice versa)? Can you say a lot in a few interesting words? I am an artist, architect, designer, consultant, lawyer, banker, politician, marketer, or reporter—sounds boring.

In essence, do you have a short description or presentation of what you do that grabs attention? If not, I suggest you to develop one, because you will meet the most influential and well connected people within and outside your profession, at places, times and moments when you least expect it. In an elevator, you could bump into 'the legendary CEO' of a reputed company you would die to work for. On a flight, you could be seated beside a renowned writer, social activist, photographer, philanthropist, consultant, academic or entrepreneur. At the lobby of a hotel, you may see a media

In 30 seconds tell me why I should hire you?
As a 'digital age' integrated media specialist, my model will clock a CAGR of 50% for your business. Hire me or somebody else will.

baron in conversation with a colleague. You have to seize your moment. Thirty seconds is all what you have to use the power of 'interesting words and sentences' to engage the important person to have a conversation with you.

You have to make the first few seconds count even if you are nervous or frightened. An elevator speech is an opportunity to make a concise sales pitch that lasts for less than a minute to captivate the eminent, celebrated or famous, to provide you an opportunity to be counted or receive advice that can change the course of your life. Fortune and luck can come knocking at your door anytime. Take the elevator ride from the first floor to the top floor today, and be prepared with your elevator pitch... In the autumn of 2005, my elevator speech opened up an unexpected opportunity for me.

It was a Monday morning; I had woken up late and groggy. I had to dash to get to class (Northwestern University) on time. Every minute mattered, and when I got to the McCormick Tribune Center (my class was held here), I had no option but to scurry for the elevator. As I hurriedly stepped into the elevator, I heard the name 'Lee Heubner.'

Lee Heubner was being introduced to a graduate student by a distinguished faculty member at Medill School. All three of them had got into the elevator before I did. Just when the doors were about to close, I managed to get into the elevator, with Chai Tea Latte and a cheese sandwich in one hand, and my heavy backpack (contained my laptop, books from the library, and a small box of delicious After Eight Mint Chocolate) in the other hand. You can well imagine how 'full my arms and hands were.'

My eyes popped out when I heard the name Lee Heubner. An alumnus of Harvard University and Northwestern University, *Lee Heubner* was the publisher and CEO of the Paris-based International Herald Tribune. He had also served as deputy director of the White House writing and research staff during US President Nixon's administration. Among other accomplishments, Lee was former president of American Chamber of Commerce in France.

In the elevator, luck smiled at me. Seconds later, the faculty member and the graduate student got off at the second floor. Lee was heading to another floor. Only he and I were in the elevator. You know how eager and energized you feel when you are in the presence of an eminent personality. After all, it is not every day you meet a person who has worked for the President of United States, is an alumnus of distinguished universities, and has excelled in various capacities. I seized the moment to introduce myself as a 'marketing, business and communications specialist who loves to write about people, relationships, products and services.' My elevator speech was succinct and caught his attention.

The affable Mr. Heubner remarked, "You must now do two things—author a book, and learn how to write and deliver speeches. Authors are often called to make speeches."

"Incredible advice," I told myself.

Lee had just opened my mind to an added opportunity for an author and writer. My elevator speech and an unexpected tryst with Lee Heubner lay the foundation for futuristic accolades, unknown to me then. He had altruistically tipped me towards speechwriting and I promised myself that I would do so one day. Little did I realize the opportunity was round the corner?

The last quarter at Northwestern University had commenced, and I had already enrolled for the courses I would pursue before graduation in December 2005. But destiny had another plan. Providence has a strange way of taking you to where you ought to be for a larger purpose. What ensued within the next *4-5 hours* had never happened to me during my academic sojourn at Northwestern University. I had planned and God smiled.

In the afternoon, as I made my exit from the computer laboratory, I chanced to meet with a classmate Michele Silverman. Michele mentioned her enrolment into an interesting course—*'Issues Management and Speechwriting.'* She suggested I enrol into the course as well. Michele's confidence always rubbed onto me. Her ability to communicate the most difficult things rather simply is her biggest strength.

I improved my persuasion and selling skills because of Michele's outstanding tips during my stint at Northwestern University. She invariably, spoke her mind and would give me an honest opinion if I ran anything by her. Michele's suggestion on the speechwriting class was well intentioned. But I had already made up my mind and enrolled into the requisite classes for the quarter.

Half an hour later I was in the student lounge, where I unexpectedly ran into another classmate Kerry E Lenahan (now Kerry Y Fede). Kerry and I had worked together in the spring quarter on a number of statistical software based assignments for a database marketing course. Her analytical skills were outstanding and few know as well as Kerry 'where' the goldmine is in the data and how to develop a connection between convoluted data output and customers' needs. Thereafter, she crafts a customized marketing and communications strategy. I was lucky to work with Kerry for an entire quarter where she taught me through the lens of statistical software, the key insights of data gold mining and subsequent linkages with effective marketing and communications strategies.

We had our lighter moments too as we exchanged funny stories from our lives, pulled each other's leg, and indulged in creative experimentation with the statistical software based assignments. Thanks to Kerry, we completed some tough and intensive analytical assignments in a lighter vein. Our intent was serious, except that we had a lot of fun in the completion of the challenging task. Kerry taught me how even the most overwhelming project could be completed with a smile and humour.

No surprises that today she helps companies and non-profits communicate their message effectively and have better conversation with their customers, donors and audience. Kerry has worked with AOL, Revolution Health, and Culture11, and possesses 10 years of varied experience encompassing marketing and communications strategy, online marketing, market research and message development. Her work has helped to further the goals of online media businesses and has lead to successful outcomes for more than a dozen national political candidates and public policy initiatives.

Kerry is passionate about providing access to education and health, and protecting the environment. She currently serves on the Board of Directors at the Academy of Hope, an adult education school, and has also provided communications strategy and professional services for the CENIT School in Quito, Ecuador. Kerry's curiosity about diverse cultures and their way of living has taken her to various international destinations; and yes, she visited India in 2008.

Back to the autmn of 2005. At the student lounge, as I got coffee from the vending machine, Kerry called out to me, 'Pushpendra you must join the speechwriting course. Different occasions call for different speeches, and since you will be globetrotting someday as a renowned professional, you should join the class.' I rolled with laughter at the 'globetrotting professional' *forecast* and knew that Kerry was just being her usual self—nice and kind.

An hour later, I unexpectedly happened to meet my classmates Angela Piercy and Heidi Thompson waiting outside the elevator on the third floor of the McCormick Tribune Centre. We exchanged notes on the courses each of us had enrolled for. Angela smiled and said 'Pushpendra why is the gifted writer in you not a part of the speechwriting course. Lee Heubner is teaching the class and few are as good as him when it comes to speechwriting.' Heidi supported Angela's recommendation. But what startled me was the name Lee Heubner. Did I hear Lee Heubner was teaching speechwriting at Medill School, Northwestern University? Which planet did I live in to be oblivious of this fascinating development? After all the same morning, I had met Lee Heubner in an elevator and he did not say anything about the speechwriting course. What was going on? Within the same afternoon, I had unexpectedly run into Michele, Kerry, Angela and Heidi, and each of them brought up the speechwriting class with me.

In the past such an occurrence had not happened to me during my time at Northwestern University, and neither was I going to be of any help to these ladies in the speechwriting class (Heidi and Angela did not take the speechwriting course). Man plans and God smiles... and that afternoon an important development was beginning to germinate for me.

I took my elevator trip with Lee Heubner and the unexpected rendezvous with four gracious ladies as a cue from the Almighty. In the nick of time, I dropped out of a class (the same class I dashed for on a Monday morning) and swapped it for the 'Issues Management and Speechwriting' class.

Coming events cast their shadows before. I realized much later that this was the divine pre-cursor of my selection as a student speaker to make the conclusion speech amidst a large gathering at the graduation ceremony of the Medill IMC programme at Northwestern University in December 2005. Graduation ceremony is big in US, akin to possibly an engagement or marriage ceremony in India. It was one of the biggest moments of my life, and the credit for this goes to a merit based education system at Northwestern University.

The speechwriting class meant writing and delivering speeches on different topics, most of which were in a US-centric context. Professor Lee Heubner was brilliant, and as he and Professor Clarke L. Caywood (Sector Head, PR and Corporate Communications, Medill IMC Programme) critiqued our written speeches and delivery, we only got better. The accomplished, Prof. Caywood had worked in politics as a speechwriter and assistant to a former Wisconsin Governor.

Given the invaluable experience of the duo, and their generosity in sharing with us some of the most unbelievable and amazing stories that shaped them as outstanding speechwriters, I knew I had all the *ingredients* to become a versatile speechwriter some day in the future.

Destiny knew that I would be selected to deliver the conclusion speech at the graduation ceremony and emerge as an author shortly. Subsequently, I have written and delivered speeches.

I had an elevator speech ready when I took the momentous elevator ride with Lee Heubner on a Monday morning in fall 2005. His advice opened up an unexpected world of opportunity for me - author, speechwriter and speaker.

Prepare your elevator speech bearing in mind that you are 'different, unique and a brand' that can redefine the world around you. You have been created for a reason and your call is to discover the true purpose of your being. Remember to make it big; 'You the brand' does not have to be dishonest or a tool of deception. On the contrary, you must be genuine, honest and true to yourself - therein lies the 'heart' of marketing wisdom.

You never know where and when you could meet your Lee Heubner. It could be in a mall, car parking, hotel lobby, rest room, friend's house, on a flight, or an event; and yes never rule out a small elevator ride. But before that ask yourself do you have an elevator speech?

***

19. Pursue What You Love—Create a Bang

He is a wonderful individual, great communicator and a thorough professional. He grew up in the US (California, New Jersey and Illinois) and Middle East, and for the last fourteen years, has lived in the city of Chicago that is home to Barack Obama, President of the United States. Anup Samanta my classmate at Northwestern University shares a special bond with India and is proud of its rich culture and heritage (hear him speak Bengali and you will be spellbound). Anup and I really got to know each other midway into the academic sojourn.

Anup has worked in marketing and sales roles for different U.S. based business-to-business and business-to-consumer organizations. His edge as a marketer comes from being equally comfortable with strategic management, quantitative and analytical disciplines. Anup is very passionate about the field of marketing and its capabilities to build corporate and product brands. His amazing insights on 'building an individual as a brand' extend to both the mainstream and non-mainstream profession. I have personally and professionally benefited from his marketing and branding counsel.

The adroit understanding he brings to marketing and branding comes from his belief that the art of true differentiation comes from the pursuit of unusual methods or novel measures leading to accomplishment of goals out of the ordinary. Anup is very well-read, which possibly explains why he has a way with intelligent queries, and when he asked me an unexpected question, which I should have been ruminating about, he made me rediscover one of my big dreams.

Anup queried, "Pushpendra, do you have an interest, avocation or craft that you are ardently passionate about and can pursue it endlessly for 12-15 hours a day without any exhaustion."

Sometimes it is the simple questions, which make you ponder your forgotten dreams and remind you of the great thoughts of the learned and the wise. Anup was alluding to the sage words of the famous Chinese teacher and philosopher—Confucius, who once said, 'Choose a job you love and you will never have to work a day in your life.'

My answer was spontaneous, 'I enjoy words and writing, and even if I wrote incessantly for 12-15 hours a day I would not get tired. I have been fortunate to have a high acceptance rate in writing. Someday I plan to write a book.'

Anup's discerning inquisition stayed with me. I realized that my love for writing was beyond minutes and hours. But it needed a structure, and what better way to eventually live the words of the great Confucius than to author books. Anup's incisive intellect also threw light on an important facet—develop your passion, hobby or avocation to such heights where you can turn it into a full time profession. And this can happen only when you 'enjoy or love' what you do and are prepared to work fervently to attain a state where you do not have to work a day in your life.

'What goes up must come down.' This proverb describes nature's unwritten law that no nation, corporation, stock market, or distinguished individual will always remain at the top. With every rise a fall is inevitable and for every boom there is bound to be a period of gloom. Thus, smart young minds are advised to take a cue from nature's dictum and prepare for the tough times when the going is good. And you can assuage the negative outcome of the rough period with your love, interest or passion.

In times of prosperity, no matter how busy your academic or work schedule looks like, take out a few hours each week, and pursue an avocation, interest or hobby that you enjoy or love. It could be something that you have indulged in the past, is a stress-buster and you are proficient in or that comes naturally to you. If you love photography get the dust off your camera and capture the moods of people in the city. If you enjoy music hone your guitar or violin skills this weekend. If salsa and tango make you dance to their tunes, indulge in it for a few hours this week. If writing is your first love, start writing about what you know best or your experiences. If gaming is your passion, try and create the ultimate game never quite seen before. If history is your fascination, figure out if the past can predict a road map to the future. If fashion intrigues you, try your hands in designing a pair of jeans for your use. The list is endless, and you only have to use your imagination to get rolling with your apparent or dormant interests.

Remember you only have to choose one avocation, hobby or interest, work on it zealously, develop it to the point of proficiency, and then turn it into a full time creative or independent venture. You can then be your own master, see through periods of economic downturn without having to worry about layoffs and pink slips.

If your weekend avocation or part-time hobby can turn into full time money generating creative or business venture, you could hire people to work for you. Additionally, your personal social responsibility goals for the small world would have been largely fulfilled, because for every job you create you feed on average 2-4 mouths, which to my mind is another form of philanthropy. Philanthropy can start with 'avocation or hobby' based entrepreneurship.

Imagine a scenario where your hobby can pay for the food and bills of a jobless in a small world. You will have an inexplicable smile on your face. Starting today approach your avocation, hobby or interests with a creative and business minded disposition—creative because it will lead to innovation and breakthroughs, business minded outlook because that will lead to 'money and employment' generation.

At the end of this chapter, I want to leave you with a few questions. Whether you are a young professional or in high school, college, or university, I want you to ask yourself these reflective questions in silence or at a quiet place and be true to yourself. Should you wish, you can seek assistance from self-help books, a career coach or close friends (not family) to arrive at an answer, but please record, capture or write your answers as you read on:

- What is that one single interest or endeavour that comes to me naturally without trying?
- What would be that one avocation, hobby, interest or career choice I 'enjoy or love,' and would pursue passionately, if I did not have to work for money or worry about it?
- Do I have any latent skill or talent that needs to be ignited?

- Which, special attainment made me stand out in a crowd, even if that happened once?
- Do I love what I pursue or intend to pursue, because it provides or will provide me money, fame, power, status or self-fulfilment?
- Who achieves greatness—people who play safe or take risks?

If you think you have the answers, pursue the path that is closest to your heart, passion or intuition. Follow the advice of business consultant, Les Brown, 'Find out what you want and go after it as if your life depends on it.'

Why? Because eminence and greatness comes through the pursuit of what you truly 'enjoy or love.' When you get to where you truly belong, you will create an impact far beyond what you have imagined.

★★★

Chapter 3

Life Visioning, Dreaming Big, Unconventional Risks and Clout of Communicators

Chapter 3 Life Visioning, Dreaming Big, Unconventional Risks and Clout of Communicators

Envision 2025 and Your Place in History

"Don't let someone else create your world, for when they do they will always create it small."

—*Edwin Louis Cole*

"Anytime you become a better communicator, you're going to become a more successful individual."

—*Sheryl Block*

20. Life Visioning—Start with a Dream and Draw it

I first met the fascinating couple—Long and Freddie Pineda in 2007. Freddie and Long are the main proponents of Effective Parenting at the Ateneo de Davao University—High School Department in Davao City, Philippines, and have been conducting Parenting Seminars for more than 10 years. Freddie is a businessman who considers running the family-owned bank as work, and managing his three branch restaurant as a passion. Long Pineda is CEO and President of two banks in the Philippines that are both pursuing microfinance. She is a fitness buff and has been a competitive mountain biker and power lifter. Freddie and Long have often been invited to speak to graduating high school students on how to plan their future. '*Life Visioning*' is the tool they have used effectively to help young minds envision their future.

All big men dream. Draw your dream today. Draw what you would like to be in ten years and then pursue it zealously.

"Draw your dream. We ask young people to draw what they would like to be in ten years—for a 15 year old this means drawing what he or she would like to be when they are 25 years old," Long said.

I inquired, "Why draw?"

"Not everybody is gifted with the talent for putting into words what one aspires to be, but every individual can draw, be it Van Gogh-type figures or simple matchstick illustrations. Even as toddlers the first attempts we all have made at trying to communicate using a crayon, pencil or pen have always been in the form of doodling or freeform drawings," Long answered.

Long continued, "My advice to young people is to draw what you would like to be; how you see yourself in ten years time. Draw your dream for yourself. Draw your dream so you have something to aspire to. Do not let constraints prevent you from dreaming. It is only when one has a dream that one then moves in a more purposeful manner to achieve the dream. If you are aware of what you aspire for, all of your actions will be geared towards achieving that future dream.'

'But a young mind with little means may not be able to dream?' I commented.

'If you would like to be a doctor but your parents do not have the financial means to send you through medical school, explore alternatives, so you can achieve that dream—excel in high school so that it will be much easier for you to get a scholarship. If you would like to earn your first million by the age of 25, plan out how you intend to get there—this means your decision on what college course to take should be geared at getting you that first million by age 25.'

'Always have a big dream—aspire to be better than what you are today. If your parents have the means to help you achieve your dreams, then you are lucky. Nevertheless, always keep in mind that at the end of the day, your future lies in your hands and only you can shape your future. So, dream your *'grandest dream'* for yourself, because your future always starts with a dream,' Freddie Pineda replied.

'Young minds in college, university or who have just started out their careers are best advised to dream big about a pursuit they love. They will then look forward to each day as the start of something new. If you decide to go into business, go into a business that you will enjoy and understand—you will always be hands-on. A famous Filipino saying goes, 'water only flows out of a water pump if you pump-prime it with water'... Success in your business will happen if you pour resources (time, strategic effort, and money) into it, but greatness will happen if you add a tinge of big dreams and passion to the venture. Draw your dreams today,' Long Pineda articulated.

Draw your dream today that counts the possibilities and ignores the impossibilities, that overcomes self-imposed limitations and alludes to lofty heights, and that draws on your passion to create an impact far beyond what you have imagined. Draw your dreams, dream your dreams and then pursue them zealously. There is nothing better than living your dreams. And you could open the door for many. For every dark night you accost in this journey of living your dreams, remind yourself of the famous words of former U.S. President, Woodrow Wilson, "All big men are dreamers."

***

21. Unproven Entrepreneurs Can Create History—Vision and Bold Dreams is the Key

"Vision is the art of seeing things invisible."

—Jonathan Swift

Infosys, Apple, Google, YouTube, Microsoft and Facebook have one feature in common. They were started by unproven entrepreneurs—individuals who had a fire in their belly and a grand vision of transforming the world around them. The

Apple, Google, YouTube, Microsoft and Facebook have one feature in common. They were started by ***unproven*** entrepreneurs.
YES!!! The inexperienced me will now leverage the internet, hi-tech and mobile world to create my international online retailing venture.

founders of these renowned companies had to face their share of challenges. Yet, they did not recoil from climbing the highest mountain. They created their own experiences and knowledge bank. To millions of individuals and entrepreneurs around the world, they are the epitome of courage, innovation, creativity and achievement, because they visualized a future that few could imagine or act upon, and dared to make a difference.

Most of the promoters of these iconic companies had little work or business experience and yet they created their own business models without being coloured by the usual cant, 'Get some real world work experience before you turn an entrepreneur.' Oscar Wilde countered this argument and said, "Experience is simply the name we give our mistakes."

While most recommend acquiring some 'real world work or business experience' before starting out on your own, the 'internet, hi-tech and mobile world' has made it possible to reverse the majority opinion—teenagers and young adults with no experience can today get into business with an innovative or path breaking idea and little capital. You learn as you do. Mistakes are commonplace, but you find your own ways of dealing with them.

When there are no pre-conceived ways of executing a task, ingenuity comes through effortlessly. You execute on instinct, and challenge conventional business logic with a new-fangled approach. You are ready to be castigated by the old and tested, but you know that the new and the untried will create their own paradigm. Devoid of the baggage of the past, and full of youthful exuberance and ideas, you the 'Lapnetmobile' generation has coalesced laptop, internet and cellphone to become a smarter, sharper, better informed, gizmo savvy, pro-risk and more determined cohort than any generation that has graced Mother Earth.

As never before, the small world, presents for its young minds multitude choices and opportunities. As long as you have a grand vision and dare to dream bold, extraordinary attainments without proven experience is possible. The ubiquitous Google, Facebook and YouTube that have become an integral part of our lives exemplify notable innovations and global acceptance with unproven entrepreneurial experience.

Ask yourself a question—which products or services are among the best known brands in the world today? I bet you have the answer faster than I can write it. No prizes for guessing. They are Google, Facebook, YouTube, Twitter, Second Life, iPhone and iPod. Most of these brands were created by companies that were started by unproven and/or young individuals. You can be the next Steven (Steve) P. Jobs, William (Bill) H. Gates, N.R. Narayana Murthy, Nandan Nilekani, Sergey Brin, Larry Page, Mark Zuckerberg, Steve Chen, Chad Hurley, Jawed Karim, Philip Rosedale or Jack Dorsey—as long as you visualize and believe that you can touch the lives of millions of people across the world.

Close your eyes, envision 2025 and your place in history. Envisage your creation of a smart phone or tablet PC that will surpass iPhone, Blackberry or iPad in terms of popularity. Dream of going beyond Steve Jobs, Bill Gates, Larry Page, Sergey Brin, Narayana Murthy, Nandan Nilekani, Mark Zuckerberg, or Steve Chen. Visualize your dream of becoming a world renowned architect, painter, designer, photographer, writer or musician. Picture the mental map to emerge as an outstanding 'young philanthropreneur' (entrepreneurial approach to philanthropy for a better world) that does the small world proud.

Remember, your life-size imagination and intrepid actions will determine your pre-eminence, and spur you towards greatness. It will happen as long as you believe in yourself, your grand vision and bold dreams. And should you ever falter, you are well advised to keep in mind the wise words of Ovid, the famous Roman poet, 'Both fortune and love befriend the bold.'

***

22. Big Dreams = Repeated Failures + Reject Rejection + Vary Approach

As you envision a great future, you must remember that even the best and proven stumble. You are no exception. People who achieve their big dreams usually experience repeated failures along the way. Mistakes become their second name and that may happen to you as well.

Fear of failure and rejection is one of the most important characteristics that 'prevents' many people from moving forward —starting their first independent venture; making a third attempt at self employment after the first two did not work out; accepting a high risk role in a job never attempted before; taking on a leadership role where the possibility of success is a mere one percent... the list is endless.

But most are not prepared to jump off the cliff, because temporary setbacks have chained them up or life in the safety zone is the preferred option—why rock the boat when all is well? Conventional thinking eschews risk taking and rewards small thinking or safe options, In the comfort zone you play safe and mistakes are small. So you lose less. Guess what—you lose less, you attain less.

I have often wondered and at the risk of being censured, I wish to put a question to all the safe players, 'How many 'play safe' people or 'small dream' individuals do you know of that have made an impact on our society? Can you think of even half a dozen men or women of note who have achieved greatness without a combination of dreams, risks, mistakes, failures, determination, perseverance and courage? I bet you cannot.

The small world is fraught with a variety of 'social pressures.' This omnipresent facet holds back big dreams, differentiated starts after repeated failures, or a foray into the risky world of entrepreneurship. Venturing into unexplored territories by defying traditional norms is a daunting task. Today, when an individual quits a highly paid job to venture into the unknown world of entrepreneurship, he or she may be considered a

My first three ventures failed. But laurels come after setbacks and failures. I bounced back with a bigger dream and today my company has a presence in 30 countries across the world
WORLD

fool by many. The ambient society prefers to reduce the risk-taking ability of an individual. By 2025 this phenomenon will undergo an immense change. Repeated or some type of failure and risk will be a pre-requisite on your résumé or CV. Failures will be viewed as a learning experience and a positive attribute. The mantra for achievers in 2025 will be—If you have not failed, you cannot move from good to great. Prepare yourself for the future. Risk failure, but do not cease your quest for greatness, glory and triumph. Step into untapped domains and pave the way for many to follow.

My fellow young friends and colleagues, you must always remember that greatness comes after setbacks and laurels after disappointments. Mistakes and failures will happen, but even the best stumble because we are human. Around the world, in different eras, history is replete with stories of great people who made innumerable mistakes and failures.

These legendary folks made sure they 'profit' from their mistakes or failures. They did not drown in despair, dwell on the blunders ad nauseam, or build a monument of their debacle. They moved on with fortitude and life provided them yet another chance to attain greater heights. You too can take a cue from them

If things do not work out the first time, start again with a fresh approach, should it muck up the second time, initiate a different technique or vary your method, and if success eludes you the third time around, adopt some other strategy or an uncommon course of action. It may not be easy, but bounce back with a 'novel, new or alternative' plan each time the attainment of your big dream is in jeopardy. If you are not convinced by my words, please go and read *The Psychology of Achievement* by Brian Tracy. He writes about four millionaires who hit it big by age 35. But it did not happen easy. Each of them was involved in an average of 17 businesses before finding the one that took them to the top. They tried and changed till they found the 'appropriate or right fit.'

Reject the rejection, negativity and gloom surrounding failures, after all this too shall pass and you would have gained valuable experience for futuristic conquests.

When you observe that every achiever destined for big things has to go through the mandatory route of failure before triumph, you can knock the feeling of dejection and keep your chin up.

Remember, those who rise from the ashes are destined to rule... provided they see failures as temporary, are prepared to modify their approach, rebuff the pessimism, and never give up on their bold dreams. After all:

Big Dreams = Repeated Failures + Reject Rejection + Vary Approach.

***

23. Unconventional Risks Create Lasting Impressions—Best Taken When Young

Risks are not boring. They are an assortment of multi-dimensional flavoured choices and options that involve change, doubt, uncertainty, and insecurity. Almost, every decision by design or unknowingly involves an element of risk. To do or not to do is also a risk. The risk of taking the next risk or the risk of status quo is also a risk.

But the risks that get highlighted are the 'unconventional' choices—you could quit a well paid job to go back to study. You could change industries when well entrenched in your present job or business. You could move within an organization to a less glamorous role only to enhance cross-functional skills. You could alter time-tested methods of doing business in your company that worked for the last three decades. You could chuck a great job to turn into an entrepreneur. You could switch from a fast track corporate career to a full time non-mainstream profession as creative writing, painting or photography. You could give it up all and move from a for profit company to a non-profit organization. You could continue to 'date or wait' till you find your 'right fit' partner, or alternatively, get married 'under family duress, for money, for looks or to comply with accepted norms.' These risks can make or mar your personal and professional life... but unusual picking, uncharacteristic choices and uncommon decisions invariably exert a long term influence over people and society.

The younger you are the easier it is for you to walk the unexpected path—strange are the ways of life. The corridor of unconventional risks can come knocking at your door much later in life. You can better handle the atypical perils if you have lived the aberrant risks when young.

In the late 1980s, my father Vijay S. Mehta was asked to 'set up and head' the credit card division at ANZ Grindlays Bank, India (it used to be the largest foreign bank in South Asia). Until then all cards in India were charge cards.

The bank wanted a heavyweight to head the profitable credit card business. In a country where credit was considered a dirty word, telecommunications were at its infancy, access to skilled consumer lending or credit card professionals was almost non-existent, there was no credit bureau or localized credit scoring model, setting up a credit card division (from scratch) then to cater to the Indian consumer was a huge risk. As if this was not enough, he was expected to launch a nationwide product with meagre resources. The mandate was to show profits in less than three years. It is public knowledge that credit card business is capital and technology intensive that takes on an average three years to break even.

My father was on the horns of a dilemma. He had a cautious corporate and branch banking mindset, and knew little about the credit card business. He was given to understand that managing risks of a credit card business may be more complicated than managing big ticket corporate loans. But he had a choice. He could have turned down one of the biggest challenges of his career and got somebody else to take up the mantle. It was a time when he was well entrenched within the banking fraternity. He had children who were in school. He knew that the odds to succeed were stacked against him and if he botched it, his career would be scarred and perhaps over.

While he could turn to advice to his trusted colleagues and friends within the financial services industry, the decision had to be his own. In a long time he felt alone and lonely. It was a tough call. The probability of succeeding was remote and he felt he was inches away from marring his banking career. Yet, the true leader dwelling within goaded him to cut the Gordian knot. He rose to the occasion, took up the challenge and in the late 1980s, successfully pioneered and launched the first credit card in India—ANZ Grindlays Bank Credit Card.

Every risk provides an opportunity, and every opportunity provides another opportunity. In 1993, my father quit ANZ Grindlays Bank to start another first of its kind; this time India's first credit card and plastic money consultancy service —Credit Card & Management Consultancy. The advisory service has been a part of varied assignments from reputed organizations within India, US, Canada, Australia, Germany, among other nations.

The consultancy service has also found regular coverage in prominent publications of the country (*The Economic Times, The Times of India, Indian Express, Business Today, Business India, Business Standard, The Financial Express,* etc.) and overseas.

Some years ago, a senior banker with a prominent financial services organization remarked, "Mr. Mehta you are the grandfather of the credit card business in India. We have a lot to thank you for. You set the trend and India is on its way to becoming one of the most exciting credit card and plastic money markets in the world. You should be proud of yourself."

Dad can look back with a lot of satisfaction because with the introduction of credit cards, he sowed the seeds for making the life of millions of Indians rather 'convenient' be it travel, entertainment and retail sojourns, crisis, emergency and medical management, utility bills payment or education fee payout.

Dad has since advised me, "You can take career defining 'unconventional' risks even on a job. Uncommon risks are not the sole purveyor of entrepreneurship or a one time act. However, it is best to take the 'exceptional' big risk when young and below 40. If it does not pay off, you would still have 10-15 important years to re-work your career."

Remember it is natural to play safe, but if you can avoid the herd mentality, stretch beyond what you think is possible and embrace the unusual risk, particularly when young, it will hurt less if it does not work out as planned. However, if it does pan out as envisaged, the younger you are, the more likely you are too be the vanguard of change.

***

24. The Clout of Communicators—2025 will Belong to Deft Communicators

Recently, I had the opportunity of reconnecting with Amisha Shah my classmate at Northwestern University. If you spend more than half and hour with her, I guarantee that your stomach will start hurting because of her incredible sense of humour laced with a terrific communications style.

Amisha can enunciate the most complex issue through the use of simple and appropriate words intermingled with an incredible sense of timing, effortless style of delivery and the requisite poise of an adept communicator.

Amisha works as a Communications Consultant to various large organizations in the Chicago area. Prior to this role, she was with Hewitt Associates, an internationally renowned human resources consulting company, where she provided strategic communications and employee communications support to Hewitt's shared services area. This included supporting the Chief Security Officer, and security and risk management function.

Describe tomorrow's 'influential' communicator?
The future will belong to simple, clear, concise, and compelling communicators drien by video and virtual based communications.

Amisha also spent six years with Accenture, leading communications and change management efforts for its clients. She completed her Bachelor's degree in Psychology and Speech Communications from the University of Illinois Urbana-Champaign in United States. Amisha exudes a passion for influencing the bridge that connects business results and people so that she can help contribute to an organization's growth, while remaining mindful of and smart about its key asset—people. She lives by a thought-provoking credo—take in the little things in life when you get a chance.

For an accomplished communications professional endowed with an ability to make meaningful 'connections,' Amisha is among the most remarkable young communicators that I have met in my life. Her success warranted me to request her to answer an important question, "What is the significance of communications for young minds and how can one perfect it as an art?"

Amisha was generous enough to pen her thoughts for the benefit of young minds. I produce her discerning write-up below.

Why Communications Should Matter

It's amazing how powerful the term 'communications' is, yet how little it has traditionally been valued as part of everyday business or personal interactions. Fortunately, this belief is evolving in the 21st century, where it is becoming increasingly important to communicate effectively as part of our normal responsibilities. Although thousands of MBAs are employed into the market each year with valuable skills as finance, marketing and general management, some may not understand what it takes to be a successful communicator and why it even matters.

While certain skills and talents can be learned on the job or trained, communications is not one that easily falls into this category. It really is much more an art than a science, and comes from within, rather than from outside influences. To add to this complexity, there are numerous cultural nuances, demographic elements and other factors to take into account when trying to 'learn' how to communicate effectively. However, that is not to say that any person can't work towards enhancing their communications skills and styles, be it professionally or personally.

There are several areas that young professionals can focus on to be ahead of the curve and position communications as an additional forte on their résumés or even in personal relationships. A successful communications 'toolkit' contains several facets, but we'll focus on three fundamental areas:

- Sharp verbal and written communications skills.
- Adequate nonverbal communications skills.
- Basic knowledge around, which types of vehicles prove most effective to deliver communications messages to target audiences.

The Communications Journey

It's no secret that the delivery of a powerful message can really impact the credibility and impact of an individual. Most recently, we can look at the example of United States President Barack Obama. His inherent charisma and grace was certainly magnified by his ability to work with his speechwriters and formulate inspiring and comforting words for millions of Americans. Further, his ability to deliver these words with confidence and fierce engagement, not arrogance and staleness, has probably marked him as one of the greatest orators of our time. Although it does take some natural ability to be as polished and influential a speaker as President Obama, it also takes the determination and understanding to make communications a priority in your agenda. This is true whether it is a business venture, a personal goal, or a political campaign.

'Simplicity and clarity' in oral and written communications will be key characteristics of tomorrow's outstanding communicator. The most potent words will be expressed succinctly and creatively with an understanding of how people feel and alignment of one's remarks to that point of view. In addition, the ability to remain calm amidst tough situations, exemplified by your unruffled tone, demeanour, intonation and overall attitude will play a crucial role in enhancing your verbal and written communications skills.

There are millions of books and theories on how to deliver the way Obama did in his own right, but truly the most practical and successful way is through persistence and practice. What does this mean? Communicating well is a journey, not a destination, so delivering one good message or writing one good communication is not enough. It is something that has to be practised through everyday formal and informal channels.

More importantly, it has to be assessed by way of feedback from yourself and those around you. If your message is clear, concise, and caters to your intended audience, you are on your way to successful message delivery. Even the greatest of speakers frequently receive feedback that their message was either confusing or too trite for their target audience.

Be sure to take the time to send yourself an email before it goes out to a larger population and ensure that it makes sense and delivers your intended messages; or listen to yourself on voice mail to see if your message is clear. Best of all, practice in front of your family, friends, peers or leaders to see if you've made your point successfully.

Finally, recognize that winning communications also carry a strong element of fluidity and flexibility. There are always circumstances beyond our control that require us to change our original communications plan and messaging, but still deliver successfully.

More Than Words Can Say

Our next area focuses on everything that isn't actually spoken or written—nonverbal communications. Although, this area is often most overlooked when talking about successful communications, it truly is the essence of making or breaking message delivery, particularly in this age of virtual workforces and social media channels, where nonverbal communication is utterly critical. In fact, research shows that body language and tone transmit almost 95 percent of information to a listener or reader as compared to just words alone.

We all know from experience that misunderstandings and ruffled feathers are a common result of poor communications that are not face-to-face. For example, how many times have you sent a carefully thought-out email to a friend or colleague only to receive a one word response? Your reactions might range from confusion to anger to apathy, and hence a potentially damaged relationship. Similarly, how many times have you been on a conference call or even a one-on-one conversation with your boss or your spouse (which in some cases could be one and the same!) and felt that after asking a question, there is pure, painful silence on the other end, for what feels like years? In both of these cases, perhaps the recipient was busy and could not reply with an equally thoughtful response, or perhaps the caller on the other end was distracted with background noise and could not hear your full question. However, it takes only one instant reaction for the message to be misunderstood and for a goal or relationship to be weakened as a result.

These are just minor examples of why polished nonverbal relationships are abundantly critical to be successful in any venue. While misunderstandings can't always be prevented, we can still follow common practices when working in virtual settings or even when delivering messages face-to-face. Examples of this include being cognizant of negative facial expressions during a conversation or meeting and trying to express concerns in a more collaborative fashion. Other examples include trying to be mindful of the tone you are using when exchanging information over email. If the message is serious, maintain a serious tone, but avoid sounding blameful or overly negative. If the message is positive, allow for some humour or a sprinkle of upbeat flavour to excite your audience. Similar practices hold true for delivering a speech. If the intent is to pull your audience in, and avoid any snoring during your delivery, try to engage with them by walking around and gesturing as appropriate, instead of sitting in one part of the room with your hands folded.

Again, much like the art of putting together words successfully and then delivering them with poise and confidence, nonverbal rhetoric is also more of an art than a science, but it is critical in making the picture beautiful.

Navigating the Journey

Once you know that you need to say something, and have identified what to say—or for that matter not to say, it is unequivocally important to determine the best channel to deliver your messages. While there is no 'one size fits all' solution for how to communicate your message, it is important to think about three things: your target audience, timing, and message content.

Without taking the needs and profile of your communications recipients into mind, you could compose a flawless message only to find it end up in a black hole. One key area to evaluate in this space is social media. While social media tools are simplifying communications enormously and allowing us to deliver important information in real time, they can also work against us if not used appropriately.

Blogs, wikis, podcasts, text messaging, and social networking tools like Twitter and Facebook are truly the wave of our presence, not even our future, but if you are trying to reach the Baby Boomer (people born between 1944-1964) audience or beyond, those tools may not be as impactful. That generation may very well appreciate some print communications or good old fashioned face-to-face, live interaction—just think about your mother appreciating a phone call instead of an electronic or text message. On the contrary, you do have your 'Generation X' (those born between 1965-1980) and 'Generation Y' (individuals born between 1980 and 1994) audiences, who are perfectly fine hearing a company update in a podcast format on their media player while running on a treadmill versus wasting time in a live setting at work.

In addition to demographics, it is imperative to think about the timing and message content. If you have a really sensitive message to deliver, it is often much more successful to do so as quickly as possible, but through the most personal means—again flexibility becomes a key success factor. However, if you have a message that could wait and you are looking to 'market' the concept, it might be fun to leverage some creative mediums such as social media or even posters, billboards and other marketing tactics.

The possibilities on how to deliver a message are endless, and often the most 'fun' part of planning communications, however, it is important to put on the brakes and analyze your intended outcomes before you move too fast.

Conclusion

My write-up only scratches the surface in terms of bringing out the significance of communications and how to perfect it as an art. It truly does take practice, persistence, and some inherent passion to want to become a good communicator. Again this applies to all situations—business, personal and the like. Fortunately, there are a myriad of professional organizations, experts, books, and courses on the topic. However, nothing really helps us understand how to get skillful at this beautiful art than lessons from the past and a desire to change how we talk to one another for the future. The sign of the times is that the future will belong to communicators. Gear up for the clout of an able communicator.

***

With the march of technology, internet and smart phones, the art of communications is increasingly becoming more valuable. As an example, stroll into a computer store and you will be presented with lots of computing options and related configuration. However, like me you may wonder why computer manufacturers and its marketers cannot simplify complicated words as 'router, firewall, cookies, RAM, hard drive, or Wi-Fi,' and disseminate it in a language that is easily understood by the average user. Today, simplicity is at a premium and the future will belong to the influential communicator who is a master of 'simple, clear, concise and compelling' communications.

I have been fortunate to have sat through interviews, meetings, speeches and discussions, and on most occasions, I am surprised at how the interviewee went beyond and provided too much detail or the speaker belaboured at length. It perplexed the listeners or the audience and they lost interest. Keep it short and simple. Extraordinary communicators, marketers and speakers know this. They find a compelling message, articulate it clearly, and are aware that in a digital and knowledge based world, you can only impress people with unadorned words and expressions.

Your rise in the future will truly be determined by your ability to be a powerful 'simple' communicator. As John Kotter, an expert on leadership at the Harvard Business School opines, 'Good communication does not mean that you have to speak in perfectly formed sentences and paragraphs. It isn't about slickness. Simple and clear go a long way.'

★★★

Chapter 4

Your Choices will **Determine** Your Future

Chapter 4 Your Choices will **Determine** Your Future

The Important 2025 Choices: Friends, Boss, Employer, Career Coach, Compassionate Leadership and Chief Happiness Officer

"How far you go in life depends on your being tender with the young, compassionate with the aged, sympathetic with the striving, and tolerant of the weak and the strong. Because some day in life you will have been all of these."

—George Washington Carverm

"God gives us relatives; thank God we can choose our friends."

—Ethel W. Mumford

25. Destiny is Determined by Choices

Our choices determine our future and destiny. The choices we make or those made for us are several—academic pursuits, type of friends, career selection, who to marry, social network, team members, assets and investments portfolio, location to live or settle in... These choices and more have vast implications on the direction of our lives.

There is no denying that the choice of spouse will probably be the most important picking for an individual's accretion and happiness quotient, but that is not a part of my purview for this project.

To my mind the key choices that will determine your personal and professional growth leading up to 2025 will revolve around the 'selection' of your friends, boss, employer and career coach (as discussed in Chapter One), your readiness

I am glad I made a well informed choice to become a venture capitalist. I hope to fund renewable energy and healthcare projects.

to adopt a collaborative mindset, your proclivity to seek help, your emergence as compassionate leader, and your allegiance to happiness. When it comes to the importance of making considered choices, nothing could be more pertinent than the words of Richard Bach (author of *Jonathan Livingston Seagull*), 'Some choices we live not only once but a thousand times over, remembering them for the rest of our lives.' Your personal and professional development will require well thought-out decisions and the choices you make early in life will play a crucial role in determining the final outcome.

***

26. Friends—The New Family

An existing reality of the small world—close, special or cherished friends as a support system are supplanting 'cousins and extended family.' This may be a bitter pill to swallow for those who believed in the age old diktat, 'Cousins, relatives and extended family first and friends later.'

Today, the friends that you grew up with in school, college and university or that you befriended later, figure in your scheme of things because you have spent more time with them, you see them more often, they know you closely, you can easily speak your mind, you have shared the good and the bad with them, and there is more in common.

I too have adorable friends in India and across 18 countries. I have been purely lucky and feel blessed to have friends who are accomplished yet modest, who have an opinion yet are not judgmental, who are rich or famous, but will always stand by a not as privileged buddy, who have little but are willing to share, who are extremely successful and yet supportive of failed attempts, who have experienced pain and yet exude a sense of humour, who have lost and yet have the gall to bounce back, who have loans but have not stopped to chase their dreams, who bring a new meaning to creativity and yet do not allow themselves to be bound by it, and who live life to the fullest as much as they honour the responsibilities that come with it. It is this cherished friendship bank that is one of my greatest possessions, and I hope that when you choose a friend they too can walk with you, not in front of you or behind you. The same rules apply to you when you befriend special people.

Friends, who are achievers yet modest, hail from a distinguished family and yet are grounded, are few and far, and when you come meet one such unpretentious individual, you know it is a friend for life. I am talking about Nimisha Bajaj, scion of the famous Bajaj family of India, niece of the illustrious Mr. Rahul Bajaj and daughter of the renowned business czar Mr. Madhur Bajaj.

Nimisha and I first met in fall 2004 as classmates pursuing the same Masters degree at Northwestern University. My first impressions about her—she is snooty and reserved. Her first thoughts about me—he is very social and talkative. Both of us were wrong as time would tell.

Nimisha was careful not to disclose her famous lineage to any of the Indian classmates or to the international students. She wanted to be treated like any other individual and befriend genuine folks. In addition, she did not want her last name to become a barrier between her and some others who were not as fortunate. Having lived in Mumbai for an extended period and being clued in to the business world, it did not take me long to figure out that she was a part of the 'Bajaj' pedigree. Before her advent at Northwestern University, Nimisha had worked in Mumbai for Leo Burnett, a reputed advertising agency. She had earlier studied in Wales (UK) and Pune, and also spent a summer at New York University honing principles and practices of marketing and advertising campaign strategies.

With the passage of time, Nimisha and I became friends and movie buddies. However, unknown to her, what I admired most about Nimisha was her upbringing. Despite being member of an elite and influential family, she was rather humble, and wanted to carve her own niche. She did not flaunt her wealth or family 'connections,' and was modest with her sojourns—shopping (little retail therapy), entertainment and leisure activities.

The winter in Evanston and Chicago is harsh and severe for many international students. When it snows, it covers the pavements and the plod through the snow to get to class in time requires a strategic approach... you do not walk, you move like a snail to avoid slipping and breaking a few bones. However, Nimisha chose to live life as an average student—she could afford to drive to school, rent a car or call for a cab at will, but she chose to 'walk or snail' to school each day.

Even in and around Evanston if it meant taking long walks to run errands, she would without batting an eye lid prefer to do so rather than squander money calling a cab or renting a car. She was comfortable eating out at 'student budget' restaurants and would prefer sharing the bill with classmates when she could have easily footed the cheque. She excelled in the Masters programme, but the recommended reading books were not all *new...* she bought used books and did not fritter away money acquiring expensive syllabus books, just because her family could afford it. She attributed this moderate approach to 'freedom with responsibility' that was inculcated in her by her family. Her expensive acquisitions were a mere ink jet printer, Taboo (an amazing word and card game), DVDs (movies and music bought in India), an iPod and a decent laptop.

Since our return to India, Nimisha's unassuming nature has not changed. Her disposition does not reek of any superiority; even as she keeps the family last name a closely guarded secret among strangers and acquaintances. She feels you can discover yourself best if you always feel you are but a mere mortal willing to learn more with your feet firmly on the ground. Nimisha is young, fun, creative and a genuine individual. The last I heard from her—she has just got back after attending a friend's wedding in a village. I salute her exceptional rearing.

Young Minds, your bouquet of friends should include genuine, encouraging, dependable, smart, flexible, cheerful, positive, optimistic, creative, witty, and fun loving individuals. Friends who wear a smile amidst adversity, share jokes when low, encourage your unconventional approach, provide an anchor when you have failed, motivate you when all seems lost, and are the kind of people you want in your inner coterie.

Avoid befriending the negative and pessimistic types. They rarely achieve great heights or pursue their own dreams and are the first to circumscribe your options or criticize your arduous efforts. As a young mind you only want to hear inspiring words like, 'Yes, this can be done. It is possible, difficult but possible. Dream big or take the unchartered route.'

When others remind you that the road to your dreams is difficult and you cannot do it, your friends need to remind you that, 'Yes you can do it.' You will end of up feeling big and rearing to go.

When you choose a friend, between yourselves exchange the beautiful words of Albert Camus, 'Don't walk in front of me, I may not follow. Don't walk behind me, I may not lead. Just walk beside me and be my friend.'

***

27. Interview Your Prospective Boss

Your boss or supervisor is a very important individual. At least a third of your day is spent working for a great, average or appalling boss; to say nothing of your dreams, holidays and vacations where he or she mentally accompanies you, particularly if you have a lousy superior who you detest.

Whether, it is a long distance, virtual or same location relationship, you will spend more time working with your boss or executing his or her plans. It is important for you to enjoy working with your boss. You can only learn and grow if you have a comfortable, relaxed, collaborative or stress-free working relationship with the person in charge. He or she may have aggressive or ambitious goals, but the superior should not create a work environment that is replete with tension, indescribable pressure, undemocratic undertones or an overbearing persona. You will feel stymied and become like a bird in a gilded cage.

Thus, I always recommended to university graduates and young professionals when interviewing for a job an important yet overlooked aspect—interview your immediate boss or supervisor before accepting a job. We may be living in a world where multiple interviews are held before you are offered a job or 360 degree feedback is in vogue, but an awful boss can mar your short term career plans, which would mean loss of valuable years or deceleration in professional development.

As young minds that graduate from some of the best colleges and universities in a small world, we are eager to land up a job with our dream company or a suitable alternative. This makes a young mind edgy and the power equation skews in favour of the hiring manager or the boss.

We forget that just as we are being interviewed for a position or role in a renowned organization, the hiring manager and the prospective company is equally eager to hire the good, the best, and the brightest.

The prospective employer's future and fortunes lie in the hand of sharp young minds as you. It may be considered normal to get nervous, but what is more important for you is to treat the interview process as a series of discussions that will allow you the opportunity to know more about the employer, and more importantly the boss you will report to.

If your prospective boss or immediate supervisor is a part of the interview process, he or she may resort to hard ball tactics, a no-nonsense demeanour, or come across as a friendly, suave, curious or affable individual.

From the likely boss's persona, you must try and gauge the following aspects, before you say 'yes' to a job offer. Please read the following inquisitions and later I will apprise you how you can figure out what the probable boss is really like. Read on:

- Is the boss what he or she appears to be or is he somebody else? Who is the real boss? Can you describe him or her in a few words? Remember the obvious isn't always apparent.
- Are you in consonance with his management and leadership style?
    - » Even if the boss seems demanding, will he or she be easy to work with?
    - » Is he or she into micromanagement (control-freak) or empowerment?
    - » Can he or she delegate and yet not abrogate responsibility? Despite your best efforts if you muck up or make a conspicuous mistake, will he or she back you?
    - » Can the supervisor share his success with the team members (includes you)?
    - » Does the superior believe in new concepts and learning?
    - » Does the boss believe in cross-functional and cross-divisional mobility?
- Do you make him or her feel insecure? Trust me this happens when you have an awesome resume, hail from a better known university or are far more brilliant than age or academic pedigree can suggest.
- Does the superior have a preference for taking risks or playing within the comfort zone?
- How long has the boss taken to get to his or her current role?

During the course of the interview, a discerning boss may volunteer information and tell you something about him or her. If that dissemination exercise does not take place, you should towards the end of the interview, politely request the interviewer to tell you something about him or her. You want to know his or her story. Your body language should show that you are genuinely interested in knowing more about him or her. Build on the information you have received and muster up the courage to ask the potential boss the following questions without worrying about time issues. It is better to ask in haste than repent at leisure—after all answers to your questions will not take more than 15-20 minutes and intelligent queries will get you brownie points as well. Read on:

- What is your management and leadership style?
- What are your expectations for the job I am interviewing for?
- Outside the job, do you have any hobbies, avocation or interests?
- If I have one bad quarter how would you react?
- Where do you see yourself 10 years from now?
- What is that one attainment you are most proud of in your career or in the present role?
- Which is your favourite book?

It is very likely that till you 'live together' with your boss at the workplace, you will not get all answers to the inquisitions enumerated above. *You may get a terse explanation or strategic version*. However, sometimes a sentence or a few words are adequate to know the outlook of a likely superior.

Alternatively, if the possible boss is a master at the art of camouflage, you may only get a sketchy picture of him or her during an interview process. Yet I exhort you to ask intelligent questions and ferret out a modicum of what to expect. You can then figure out if you and your prospective boss will be the 'right fit' for each other. An insight or a quick peek into the mindset of a potential boss is better than ignorance, and can abet decision making to obviate hours of anguish or acceptance of an offer that will lead to growth and a cherished association.

Your first progress point within a reputed company is your boss. No matter how brilliant you are, if you and your boss are not an 'appropriate or good' fit, your short term career may suffer. That may mean being left behind in a competitive country. For sure, you can bounce back and emerge victorious in the long term, but why lose years and sleep, if you can figure out during the course of the interview if your boss and you will be a 'suitable' fit.

Remember to interview your likely boss or supervisor the next time you are invited to an interview with a company. You must repeat the process each time you interview for a job. The practice of 'interviewing the boss' will lead to proficiency, and what you may not get right during the first two or three interviews or the first two jobs, may hit the bull's eye with the third job.

***

28. You and Employers where Chairman or CEO Remain Unchanged for a Decade or Over

At the cost of sounding impudent, I am going to suggest to you my young friends and colleagues a career tip that will make me unpopular, but to my mind is imperative for your professional augmentation—by all means go and work for a reputed organization where the Chairman or CEO remains unchanged for a decade or more, but after you have spent 5-6 years with the organization, please quit and move on elsewhere.

I salute the contribution of certain iconic and ethical companies of the 20th century, which have made a big difference across geographic regions and varied sections of society (external customer included). But I am not sure if some of these celebrated organizations have been fair to the different levels of management (their internal customer) within the organization, because they continued with the same notable individual as Chairman, CEO, Managing Director, President, or Country Head for a decade or more.

Professionally managed for profit and non-profit organizations have examples galore, where the individual at the top continues to remain at the helm for a decade and more. Imagine a scenario where the CEO in a particular company is at the foremost job for an extended period of a decade or more. The suite of 'C' executives that report to the CEO namely CFO, CMO, CHRO or CIO will have little to look forward to in terms of promotion and would continue to report to the same individual for 3,650 days or more (I am not calculating the additional day in a leap year during this period). The top 'C' executives will continue to hold the same title or be shuffled around, and would have to wait for years before one of them is elevated to the coveted premier post of CEO.

During this period their families and they will be well looked after by their employers, but after a while this may not be enough for other ambitious suite 'C' executives. While, few top executives would candidly or publicly admit to the disappointment of reporting to the same individual for years, a veneered air of frustration will loom around in their minds (rightly so because they may be extremely capable to occupy the key job).

The result—the elite 'C' club continue to languish in hope and smug satisfaction or quit at an opportune moment for better pastures. A bank of expertise departs with such unceremonious exits and colleagues until yesterday, become competitors at rival companies.

Additionally, a wrong signal is sent to different levels within the organization when the CEO remains glued to the top job for many years. The middle and junior management considered the back bone of any organization get their perceived 'anti-growth' message—'We ask you to perform for your employers, but curtail your ambitions. You will make it to senior management, but you should be prepared not to move any further, because even the top management is 'stuck' at the same level and continues to 'strive for years' without any assurances of getting the prime job (CEO) in an organization. Next in line are the members of the senior management who compete among themselves for 'years' to make it to the top management.'

The game of musical 'power' chairs goes on. At every level, hierarchical layers are added in an organization to retain people and the flat structure turns into a 'top heavy and senior bulky' organization structure. Probe further and you will witness that politicking; nepotism and bureaucracy have set in. The organization continues to prosper because of its leadership, branding and rich legacy, as is believed by the CEO, board of directors and its management team.

What they fail to observe is the 'missed' opportunities, (including, enhanced revenue and profits) that could have come their way had the organization been a better change agent starting with replacement of the 'man at the top' at least once every decade.

Globally, a number of prominent organizations have lost great minds and talent to competitor companies, because the 'chief in command' was around for just too long. While in office, rarely do we see a 'person in charge' opt out of the topmost role (after serving for a long period of time) and make way for the second in command (N.R. Narayana Murthy of Infosys in India is a great example). 'Relinquished Succession' out of volition is the hallmark of a great leader.

After being around as CEO for a decade or over, you chose to pass the baton to your successor and bow out with dignity. Ten years or more at the top with an established organization is a long time in today's competitive world to ring in a change or make a difference in society. Life is lonely at the top for heads of organizations who overstayed their welcome. As a result, most CEOs reach out to CEOs of other organizations to form their own legion or group.

I understand that people today make it to the senior and top management a lot earlier than their predecessors in the 80 and 90s. We have a number of CEOs in our small world who have become heads of companies by the age of 35 or 40. Should they serve one organization for a mere 10 years at the top and quit at 45 or 50? Debatable as it may seem, the answer to my mind is YES. I am not saying we penalize those who make it to the coveted CEO post at age 35 or 40 by asking them to hang their boots at a relatively young working age. I am suggesting that irrespective of age, brilliance, contribution, profile, visibility, or calibre, every CEO is replaceable, and should give way to the next in command after serving the same organization for a decade or more. This will foster the strategic long term growth of an organization, enhance governance, abet innovation, lead to superior succession planning, and set true example of leadership.

I am not suggesting that you do not work for companies that may be big or reputed. By all means do so as they are a great place to augment functional capability, build a network of smart executives and work on mega projects with colossal resources. All I am recommending is that irrespective of company size or iconic stature; please do not work for more than 5-6 years with an organization where the man at the top has been around for a decade or over, because it will impede your career progression.

If big corporations or conglomerates are pragmatic in disposition (they can dump you when it suits them), you too have to be smart. 'Long serving CEO based' reputed or large companies are terrific places to make your résumé more saleable (a big brand on your résumé will open many doors for you in the future), so go work for them for 5-6 years, but as a golden rule for the 21st century, please do not spend a decade or longer at such 'larger than life one-man aura' driven companies. At the cost of falling out of favour, please heed my unpopular advice or be prepared to risk the peril of becoming deadwood by 2025.

***

29. Ask for Help

Michele Castle (now Michele Long) taught me that the smartest people ask for help and achievers associate with believers, winners, triers and positive minded strugglers (even if they have failed repeatedly). I first met Michele at Northwestern University in 2004. She and I were in the same class for all the courses in the first quarter of the IMC programme.

A percentage of our grades came from 'class contribution' i.e. what we said in class—this meant talking and sharing one's thoughts with our faculty and classmates. I was a pretty vocal contributor and did offer my two cents on discussions that went around in the class. I am pretty sure I must have said some inane things during the early days of the Masters programme, for Michele to approach me while I was working on a marketing assignment in one of the computer labs.

Michele smiled and asked me, 'How old are you. I need to know?'

I was taken aback. For a minute I wondered if I said something silly in class to upset her.

I quipped, 'You will never know. Keep guessing. I am young enough to date and old enough to be here.'

She laughed and replied, 'I will make sure I know how old you are... very soon.'

'And why may I ask,' I said.

'Because you seem a smart and positive guy,' Michele replied with a mischievous look.

I have an MBA in marketing from a top US B-school and over 20 years of marketing experience, but no idea of 'Social Media' Marketing. Can you help me?
Sure. And in turn I would love to learn more about the 'Art of Branding' from you.

I knew she was kidding and being polite to strike a conversation. Our banter lasted for ten minutes, good enough for me to know that she hailed from New York, had worked at the reputed University of Chicago, was an alumni of Dartmouth College, and thought rather highly of international students in US, particularly Asians.

Over the next few days, Michele would take playful and friendly digs at me in class and the computer lab. She seemed a bright and entertaining individual. Little did I realize then that over the next 15 months, Michele and I would become 'study buddies' strategizing on courses as diverse as statistics, analytics, marketing and finance. My grades looked good during the intensive Masters programme, but a significant share of the credit goes to Michele. And here's why. Michele knew the importance of reaching out to seek help.

Michele was a secure person and did not bat an eyelid to ask for assistance from the most 'unexpected' but suitable person in an endeavour to attain her cherished goals. She knew that to emerge as a proficient marketing and communications professional, it is imperative to acquire requisite finance skills. Michele's academic credentials were outstanding and work experience inspiring, even as she stood out as an excellent communicator. For somebody with her profile, it may not have been easy to say, 'I need help.'

The 'unexpected' person was yours truly, and when she requested me to assist her better understand key concepts pertaining to accountancy and finance, I gladly accepted, albeit I was surprised—why did she come to me for help, when I was an international student and it would make more sense for her to approach a domestic classmate to understand the nuances of US finance and accounting principles. Michele had a reason, I had international work experience, a knack to relate finance with marketing and communications, reached out to people easily, and exuded a positive energy to alleviate stressful moments.

It was a pleasure working with Michele to get her up to speed on finance. She was inquisitive, determined, demanding, hard working and challenged me with queries that made me think hard and long.

Never did she crib about accountancy or finance concepts that were difficult or alien to her, never did she give up on herself or my erratic ways of teaching, because at the core she believed that she was a winner who could achieve the most difficult task. And yes, she scored higher than me during the mid-term finance exams. Michele's upbeat attitude and hard slog had paid off, and I had got my true reward. The student had surpassed her guide.

I helped her gratis, and she voluntarily reciprocated to ease my business statistics travails. Her positive energy rubbed onto me, and slowly but surely statistics and analytics were no longer beyond me. Our close association with finance and statistics rubbed onto other areas. We started looking out for each other in other courses, varied assignments and projects.

Michele and I studied together for exams and helped iron out each others grey areas, but never wasted an opportunity to make fun of each other. We also provided each other discerning leads for futuristic career development. She was friendly with most, but very focused during the academic sojourn at Northwestern University.

Very few knew her personal mantra for success – 'Ask for help even if capable and befriend the achievers, winners, believers, triers and positive minded strugglers, even if they have failed repeatedly.' She called these people the positive folks and steered away from the negative, the excusers and the sulkers.

Michele taught me that asking for help (even if capable) was not a weakness but a sign of growth, something, which I hardly adopted as a practice with classmates in college or as a consultant at my workplace in India. She taught me the importance of asking for help from a suitable individual not only when I worked on academic assignments, but also when it came to 'real life' work projects that came naturally to me or were at my fingers end. 'You will only become a better professional,' Michele said.

Thereafter, for a number of academic courses and assignments at Northwestern University, and subsequent work related projects, I followed Michele's suggestion, and reached out to classmates and work colleagues seeking assistance to improve my skill set.

For the first time, I realized that it was easy to extend assistance, but when it came to asking for help from classmates or colleagues I did have a concealed pride. And the only way to overcome my self-imposed barbed wire of obscured vanity and improve as a professional was by soliciting aid.

In January 2006, Michele moved to the New England region in United States. She works for a diversified Fortune 50 company, and today is equally good at marketing, public relations, marketing communications, sales promotions and strategic management. Her success as a young professional comes because of an insatiable appetite for learning, her belief in associating with positive people (believers, winners, achievers, triers and positive minded strugglers), and a remarkable ability to ask for help from the most unexpected 'right' source.

In a digital world, she and I continue to seek help from each other or suitable sources to bruise our respective egos and lift our professional graph. Memorize the equation:

Asking for Professional Help = Hurting Your Ego = Professional Evolution.

***

30. You Have a Choice—to be a Caring or Self-Absorbed Leader

Before, I relive a personal story of incredibly compassionate leadership, I exhort you to keep in mind a cardinal truth: **'No exceptional leader makes it alone.'**

Caring is a competitive advantage in a collaborative world and exceptional leaders live by it...for no great leader makes it alone.

They know that caring and compassionate leadership is not just about generosity or benevolence, but also making sure that as they grow and prosper, those around them also blossom and thrive.

In the summer of 2005, I was hired by Atlanta based InfiCorp Holdings, Inc., to act as a business consultant (as a part of their team) to Scotiabank's credit card division. Scotiabank, head quartered in Toronto, Canada, is one of North America's leading financial institutions.

I was told the assignment would be quite a challenge as Canada and United States are widely divergent financial services markets with differing consumer mindset and payments pattern.

I was excited to get started with the assignment as it would allow me to comprehensively understand the U.S. and Canadian retail banking, consumer lending and bank cards market, and then recommend an integrated business approach to Scotiabank's credit card division. In addition, I was looking forward to moving to Atlanta for three months, because of its remarkable history and warm people who could effortlessly make strangers feel at home.

The consultancy assignment would have meant regular travel to Toronto, and for one with wanderlust as yours truly there could not have been a better advisory project for the summer of 2005. Christina Panay from InfiCorp was to be my supervisor for the summer. She had relocated to Atlanta a few years ago and was originally from New York.

I landed in Atlanta on a late Saturday morning. It was hot and as muggy as Mumbai, good enough for me to feel at home. From the airport I headed directly to the upscale apartment complex, where I had leased out an apartment for the summer.

The apartment was in the affluent Buckhead (considered the jewel of the city) section of Atlanta, and I was pretty sure the weekends would be packed with lots to explore. Another, major plus was InfiCorp's office location—a stone's throw from the apartment complex. This ensured my summer would be highly productive.

I was led to believe that once I had signed the lease and as per mutual agreement, the property management services at the posh apartment complex in Buckhead would set up my apartment. Thus, when I signed the lease papers (long distance), I felt sure that when I would walk into the apartment in June it would already have been set up (good to go) to my satisfaction. But a surprise was waiting for me. As I walked into the apartment with my bags, I was astonished. The place was bare... the saving grace—carpeted floors.

The apartment had no bed, not even basic furniture. I was staring at blank walls and an empty kitchen. What was going on? I had clearly mentioned my requirements for the apartment to the property management office, and they had assured me that before I moved in they would equip the place with the basic necessities that included a bed and furniture.

I went to the property management office and quizzed them about the empty apartment. It was apparent something was amiss, which kept the apartment clear and unfurnished. Our discussion led to an argument that was getting no where.

Being a Saturday afternoon, the earliest something could be done by the property management office to get the apartment ready would mean waiting for the weekend to get over. Except service apartments, there were no other apartments available in the complex I could have leased out for the summer. The ritzy service apartments required a six months lease. With a bad back, it was not possible to spend the weekend on a carpeted floor in my leased apartment. Perhaps, I could buy a sleeping bag or mattress for the weekend? Should I move into a hotel for the weekend? But as a matter of principal, why should I pay out of my pocket for the blip made by the property management office. They were not in a position to refund my weekend hotel stay.

I had no car, friends or relatives in the city... but Michele Castle's advice 'Ask for help from a suitable person,' came to my rescue.

I thought of calling Christina Panay to get help. I knew it was a Saturday afternoon and calling a supervisor who was a stranger then, was not a good idea. She may be travelling, busy doing her own thing, or simply miles away having lunch with friends. Caught in a conundrum, I reluctantly dialled her cell number to apprise her of the 'no-roof' crisis ...bingo, she picked up the phone. As luck would have it she was in office, which was barely a five minute drive from the swanky apartment complex in Buckhead. She was flabbergasted and promised to come over in 15 minutes to solve the problem. Spot on—15 minutes later she walked into the property management office and refused to accept their argument about the apartment glitch. But at the back of her mind she knew that the apartment could not be set up before Monday. So she pressed for a suitable alternative. She got it. The manager offered an expensive, fully loaded classy hotel type service apartment for my three months stay within the apartment complex. The service apartment required a minimum of six months lease, but he comprehended the goof up and was prepared to make an exception to make up. The monthly tariff was steep. It was a good $600 per month higher than the apartment rent I had signed a lease for. What Christina did next, bowled me over.

She called the CEO of InfiCorp who was away in New York and convinced him to authorize InfiCorp to pick up the additional $1,800 for the three month service apartment lease. In the past, I had worked as a consultant with a number of reputed domestic and international organizations, but this generous act for an outsider, an individual she would not see after three months, was way beyond what I had experienced. You may argue she went out of her way, because I was important for the consultancy assignment, and she was overall responsible for prudent management of a big client as Scotiabank. But to me her kind gesture was the mark of an outstanding leader.

I thought her munificence and concern would end there, but it did not. After I moved my bags into the stylish service apartment, she took me out for lunch to a plush restaurant. This was followed by a visit to Kroger (a big supermarket chain in US) to enable me to buy groceries for the following week. She then drove me around certain parts of Atlanta to provide a feel of the city that would be home for me for the next three months. The evening ended with dinner at one of the finest Indian restaurants in Atlanta. Once again Christina did not allow me to pay for the meal.

As if this was not enough, when she dropped me back to the service apartment (my new home), she handed me her Kroger card, which would give me attractive discounts each time I went for grocery shopping. Over the next three months, thanks to Christina, I saved hundreds of dollars. She also asked me to use her car on the weekends to explore Atlanta. She did not want me to fritter my money renting a car.

The characteristic of an impressive leader is the ability to influence the upper echelons of an organization, and take the risk to present an 'unknown' outsider to key personnel through one-on-one appointments or meetings. At the outset of a critical project, the leader gives a boost to the outsider and also sends a signal to the top and senior management that the unknown outsider is amidst us for an important project. Christina's meticulous disposition made sure that I spent the first week through one-on-one meetings with the top (President and CEO included) and senior management of InfiCorp, including key members of the InfiCorp team seconded to work for the Scotiabank project. This ensured a cross-functional perspective encompassing finance, consumer marketing, portfolio management, credit and risk management, recovery and collections, human resources, analytics and systems, operations and service, and client relations.

I met some of the brightest individuals who possessed years of experience acquired through stints at top financial services organizations. Within a week I grew a few years. They had the patience to answer my countless queries and equally eager to know about my perspectives on consumer banking, retail lending and bank cards (credit, debit, smart, biometric, pre-paid, affinity and co-branded), including marketing, customer loyalty, communications, financial analysis, and online fraud prevention. Exchange of perspectives meant I learnt a lot, and somewhere within I knew the summer of 2005 would be special.

Over the next 11 weeks, Christina and I developed a great working relationship. She was not a control-freak micromanager. On the contrary, she trusted me implicitly, gave me a free hand and opened up her knowledge based resources (worth thousands of dollars) to me. Christina was a great judge of people, and knew that I would never betray her faith, which is why I had 'inconceivable' access to confidential files and important online intellectual property.

While in Atlanta or Toronto, the kind of unbelievable faith she reposed on me, I knew I could not let her down. Even though Christina stayed back late at work, if I did so, she would sound me out to drop everything and head home right away. I would not heed her advice... work longer hours than she expected, and even take work back home, albeit often being admonished by her for sitting up late and sending emails pertaining to work late in the night.

She was caring, and would often check on me to see if I needed anything to make my stay in Atlanta comfortable. At the same time, she would often cajole me to use her car and save money spent on cabs. Christina kept a bowl full of chocolates and candies on the coffee table in her office room. Every morning she filled up the bowl with mouth-watering candies and chocolates, and by the same evening or next day they were over.

Office colleagues would walk into her room, strike up a conversation with her and binge on the delectable delights. I too became a victim of the scrumptious chocolates. She would get me my favourite candies and chocolates, and goad me to take some home as well.

Christina went out of her way for her team members, a fact they vouched for in her absence. She never allowed team members to spend on her, with me being no exception. At the airport, when we would wait to take a flight from Atlanta to Toronto or vice versa, I could not even buy her bottled water. At the end of the summer, she threw me an impressive farewell lunch party at a classy restaurant, which was well attended by most team members on the Scotiabank project, including the CEO of InfiCorp and friends I had made within the organization. The farewell meal was in recognition of a great job done by me over the summer, so Christina opined. But had I goofed up, she would have still thrown a warm send-off party. That is what makes Christina Panay such an able manager, deft leader and wonderful human being.

By the end of the project, she made sure I knew more, had grown as a professional and enjoyed my stint at InfiCorp. In a competitive and cut-throat business world, she is like a whiff of fresh air—Christina cares for her team members as family, she trusts them as few can, she exposes them to the best without a shade of insecurity, she looks out for them so that they are continually motivated to excel, she ensures performers willingly do not attrite to competitors, she leads from the front as she brings out the best in each team member, and should their performance wane, she uses her leadership acumen and the gift of the gab to get them on course. Christina is young (in her 30s), super intelligent, great communicator, outstanding leader... but above all an individual who creates a sense of belonging to a team and organization.

Young Minds, in a small world we have a choice as a leader —to care or be self-seeking, to empower or micromanage. You can appreciate, compliment and respect your team and colleagues or sound condescending, egotistic and abrasive. You can show courage and take hard decisions or lack the gall and opt for soft options. You can prosper and make those around you flourish, or you can build on your acquisitive tendency and amass a fortune only for yourself. You can share acquired knowledge or expertise with your team members (sharing is growing) or reserve the best for yourself. You can hire those who are smarter than you (perhaps make you insecure) or bring on board mediocre team members who make you feel secure. The former approach may be difficult to adopt in the short term, but in the long term will ensure you stand out as a leader.

The opportunity of creating a team that cares for its participants and stakeholders will present itself to you. You have an option to seize the moment and create a compassionate team that will build an extraordinary organization or develop a team that only cares about profits and callous accomplishment of goals. You have a choice to 'care and lead' or just lead. Individuals have emotions and egos, and you can make them feel important or wasted. Remember when you touch the life of a colleague; you are sowing the seeds of how you will be treated in your long career by your superiors, associates or clients.

Acts of benevolence can also happen at the work place... start today with a small kind act for people who work with and for you. Your world of tomorrow will then witness more smiles, better work environment (entrepreneurship or job), enhanced performance and lower churn rates. No great leader makes it alone. Great leaders know that legacies are created by teams, with teams, and through teams. Nurture your team and time will see the emergence of an extraordinary leader, and if you do not believe me listen to the wise words of Scott Johnson, 'Caring is a powerful business advantage.'

***

31. Allegiance as Chief Happiness Officer

At the end of our time together, I wish you to spare a few minutes and focus on the unprepared facet of our lives—the 'choice to remain happy amidst continual challenges.' I am inspired by the evocative words of Lord Buddha, 'Happiness comes when your work and words are of benefit to yourself and others.'

I am glad my book has made a difference in the lives of young minds.
I know nothing has brought you more joy than the publication of your book. It has inspired them to **dream big or differentiate** in a small and wired world.

Young Minds, as we journey on we may have to face impediments, disappointments, struggles or failures in pursuit of our bold dreams or cherished goals, but I will implore you to remember the wise words of Gautama Buddha, particularly when the going is tough, so that you can continue to move forward to attain your big dreams, make a difference and inspire people to draw strength from your example.

My classmate at Northwestern University, Chris Rathje, is a gifted writer and author of the story *The Triplet Raised* by Wolves published in the book *Chicken Soup for the Soul: Twins and More*. Amidst all his overwhelming challenges, Chris has been of tremendous inspiration to me over the last five years.

We stayed in the same residential 'dorm' apartment complex during our academic sojourn at Northwestern University, and each morning his warm smile and cheery greetings made sure I had adequate positive energy to last an entire arduous day.

Chris has been kind enough to share some of his thoughts on happiness that appear on his website—www.chrisrathje.com and provide astute suggestions to overcome struggles and keep smiling. Read on.

You are your own Chief Happiness Officer!

I just came up with this term yesterday, but I'm already a big fan. I have learned I am in complete control of my life. If there is an activity in my life that brings me nothing but negative emotions it is up to me to change the activity or eliminate it. I am my own Chief Happiness Officer. No one else can make sure I am joyful, except myself.

Your brain is an antenna

In accordance with the law of attraction, we are all truly antennas. Whatever we have going on in our minds has a way of manifesting itself in our realities. A great example of this... several weeks ago I noticed if I was in a happy mood while driving, happy songs showed up on the radio. However, times where I was feeling a little blue, sad songs had a way of appearing.

The winds of favour will blow your way—anything is possible.

The 21st century is a new age of understanding human potential. The way to succeed in life is to have the courage to keep fighting to attain your dreams, even if the road is not a straight line. Fighting is not about gritting your teeth and pulling your self through every moment. Instead have a smile on your face and charge through problems and impediments that might arise on your journey. The key is to exude the strength to overcome difficulties, and not curse the struggles. You should avoid circumscribing your thoughts to mere preservation or survival. It is not about survival of the status quo, but about the times of prosperity and greatness that lie ahead. Life is like the stock market with its ups and downs, and no matter what the 3D world tells you, keep a cheerful and positive attitude. Regardless of your surroundings the winds of favour will eventually blow your way. Growth is the objective, not perfection. Anything is possible!

Life is a team sport

Every young mind must pursue 'everything in love.' Life is a team sport. It is easy to go into survival mode and to fight and claw for the numero uno spot, but we all accomplish more when we work together. Follow the joy—if something makes you happy keep doing it and eliminate worry or fear. The right path will illuminate itself if you follow your dreams, stay positive, work well with others and wear the Chief Happiness Officer tag on your sleeves.

***

Young Minds, I have found through experience that true happiness comes primarily from commitment to a worthy or admirable purpose that is beneficial to you and others. There is a reason for all of us to be on Mother Earth, and the lives of great and renowned people from all walks and vocations of life delineate that nothing brought more joy to them than fruition of their worthy intent or laudable objective that also made a noticeable contribution to society.

Lasting happiness does not come from how important you are in society or your enormous possessions, but from positive thoughts and the pursuit or attainment of a commendable goal that also touches the lives of others. Yes, material paraphernalia is important and provides pleasure, delight, thrill, and elation, but only a worthy objective that goes beyond self-seeking aspiration can provide permanent euphoria.

You have a choice to look for enduring happiness through pursuit of a laudable or admirable goal or merely seek happiness through self-gratification. The build up to 2025 starts with your ability to think freely, your capacity to enjoy simply and the commitment to live your dreams... that brings a smile on your face when you see others beaming with a wider smile. Good luck and Congrats in anticipation.

★★★